SUSAN MITCHELL

Splitting the World Open

TALLER POPPIES AND ME

ALLEN&UNWIN

First published in 2001

Allen & Unwin
83 Alexander Street
Crows Nest NSW 2065
Australia
Phone: (61 2) 8425 0100
Fax: (61 2) 9906 2218
Email: info@allenandunwin.com
Web: www.allenandunwin.com

National Library of Australia
Cataloguing-in-Publication entry:

Mitchell, Susan.
  Splitting the world open: taller poppies and me.

  ISBN 1 86508 413 1.

  1. Mitchell Susan, 1945– . 2. Women—Australia—
  Interviews. 3. Women—Australia—Biography.
  4. Celebrities—Australia—Interviews. I. Title.

305.420994

Poem on p. 38 is from John Keats' 'Ode to a Nightingale'.

Set in 11/15 pt Adobe Garamond by Midland Typesetters, Maryborough, Vic.
Printed by Griffin Press, South Australia

10 9 8 7 6 5 4 3 2 1

For Mary, without whom
there would have been
no 'Tall Poppies'.

'What would happen if one woman
told the truth about her life?
The world would split open.'

—Muriel Rukeyser

CONTENTS

lunch

It began with a lunch. Like most of the important things in my life.

Perhaps I even began with a lunch. Perhaps my parents, Jean and Mitch, after what they would have considered a really good lunch of roast lamb, crunchy roast potatoes, carrots, pumpkin, parsnip, minted fresh peas and home-made gravy followed by Jean's apple pie and cream, perhaps they took themselves off to bed and there in the shaded afternoon silence of the suburbs, they made wild and passionate love. Made me.

Funny, you get to a certain age and the thought of your parents having sex no longer repulses you. Not like when Deirdre Polkinghorn told me what she saw her parents doing.

'Don't be ridiculous,' I said.

'Your parents do it too,' she said.

I told her that my mother and father would never stoop to such a disgusting act, that my mother had told me to look away when my dog Chips had been doing something that sounded very similar. Mum said he couldn't help it because he was a dog, and now here was silly little Deirdre chanting 'they do it, they do it, they do it'. Until I winded her.

Lunch with the publisher at one of Sydney's classiest restaurants, however, was not in any way sexual. It was much more exciting. I could smell a book proposal.

There, after the starched white tablecloth, the starched white napkins, the starched white waiters, the fresh scallops in ginger, coriander and balsamic, the lightly poached sole in a scallion and champagne sauce and several glasses of the best Sauvignon Blanc (I'm a little tired of Chardonnay, aren't you?), he, the publisher, said he wanted me to write a book on 'Women and the Millennium'.

'Oh no, not the big "M" word.'

He looked me straight in the eyes. No-nonsense, business look. 'Why not? No one has narrated or celebrated more stories about women's lives than you. The end of one century and the beginning of another. It's a very important time.'

I agreed that it was an important time.

He continued. 'It's also time for you to tell your own story, or parts of it.'

'You mean combine the two?'

'Why not?'

Several more glasses of wine and I was agreeing with him. Totally. It all made such absolute sense. Of course. It was the obvious next step. What was I waiting for? To turn eighty?

For some years, like a documentary maker, I had wanted to revisit some of my Tall Poppies. Here was my chance. Landed in front of me on a big, fat, white plate, next to the publisher's business card. 'Think about it,' he said, 'and get back to me.'

Now it's midnight. I'm totally sober. I'm doing what I always do when I'm trying to come to terms with something. Making a list.

Pat O'Shane, Maggie Tabberer, Eve Mahlab, Robyn Archer, Fabian Dattner, Anne Summers, Sallyanne Atkinson.

An interesting mix.

Why choose them?

I love survivors. People who not only never give up, but who continue to bloom. My choice probably says a lot more about me. Perhaps the publisher was right. Perhaps it is time to come out from behind the mask of the invisible, 'objective' author. Perhaps it is time to tell some of my own stories. Biographers have traditionally taken on the task of 'telling' the lives of others while revealing nothing about themselves. They habitually disappear behind their work and claim to be impartial in their judgements. What of their own lives? What about their own doubts, dreams, desires and disappointments? Their own hard truths. Don't they bring all this to their telling of another's life? What they choose to include or leave out, which bizarre or seem- ingly trivial detail is highlighted, surely tells us more about the biographer than the subject. Why not admit it?

Celebrate it.

The pursuit of truth is a fascinating and contradictory exercise.

We all know that the true account of what happened in a road accident depends entirely on which corner you happened to be standing or which car you were in, or what mood you were in, or the state of the weather, and many, many other factors, trivial or vital. On the one hand, the truth seems easy to find. Every nuance, every inflection can all be noted, the body language, the eye contact. I am like a dentist with a probe who digs and pokes until something crumbles and a tiny crack appears. I dig and poke some more until the crack is exposed as a cavity. However, unlike the dentist, my job is not to fill the cavity, merely to expose it.

On the other hand, living subjects can be difficult or devious, don masks, be spin doctors or fantasists or just plain liars. After all the sifting, the sorting, the weighing up, 'truth' comes down to the writer's own judgement. The biographer of the living is always both the seducer and the betrayer. I have written eight books of non-fiction based on words that have come from the lips of the subjects themselves. And yet, if I am honest, I know that what I choose to include, what I choose to leave out, how I decide to rephrase or rewrite their words into what appears to be a seamless monologue, is what determines at least part of the truth of their stories.

And the writer's judgement, in my case, has just as much to do with my ability to tell the truth, which, in turn, has everything to do with my own life, my own history, my own dilemmas. None of these factors is usually included in a traditional attempt to tell the story of another person's life. Usually we know nothing of the personal life of the biographer other than what we can extrapolate from the few notes at the beginning of the book, the dedication and, of course, the author's photo, usually at least ten years old and taken with glycerine over the lens.

Ideally the reader should know something about me, the writer. You should know something about the circumstances under which the information was gained, and aspects of my own life that perhaps show why I was drawn to choose these women to write about, to interpret their stories, to walk in their footsteps.

My first book, *Tall Poppies*, was an honest attempt to tell the truth about the lives of women who, against all odds, had been high achievers in their field. It was also a personal search for role models. There was no book when I was growing up that told us about such women and the real stories of their lives.

Australia has always had a problem with success. The nature of our tawdry beginnings, the rampant egalitarianism, the elevation of the group or team above the individual, the fear of superlatives, the black humour—all have conspired to make us uneasy about elevating successful individuals above others. Hence the ubiquitous 'tall poppy' syndrome. The only exception is the national obsession, sport.

By returning to the subject of *Tall Poppies* fifteen years later, exploring where they and I had been in the intervening years and were going at the turn of the century, I hoped to shed some light on the truth of the lives of women who are taking part in the action of their times. The ongoing saga of their lives and times.

I do love a saga.

The next day I rang the publisher.

Yes, I said. Yes.

PAT O'SHANE
Magistrate

Grew up poor in a tiny sugar town in the deep north of Queensland. Aboriginal mother. Irish cane-cutting father. First born of five children. Mother worked as a domestic in hotels, father frequently on strike. Education was the path out of poverty. Mother not bitter at racial slurs, just taught Pat to be tough enough to survive them. Kids often called Pat 'black gin' or 'nigger'. She used to punch them out but learned that her tongue was a stronger weapon. Her mother taught her that she was as good as anyone else, her father to question authority. She repressed the hurt and used it as a spur. In grade six she topped the class, and the teacher said to the boy who had previously come top, 'You should be ashamed of yourself, letting a girl beat you.' Pat thought, He's never going to beat me again. And he never did. Always feeling the outsider, she knocked herself out to be the best.

After ten years of teaching in secondary schools, of encountering racial pressures, bearing two children and suffering an unhappy marriage, she had a major breakdown. After four years of psychiatric treatment and fighting the recommendation of lobotomy, she went to Sydney, worked as a secretary and then became the first Aboriginal woman to graduate a lawyer. Practised at the Sydney Bar and in Alice Springs as an advocate for Aborigines.

Hates Aboriginal men who want a high media profile without doing any of the hard work. Women have been her support and power base. First head of the Department of Aboriginal Affairs in New South Wales (1984).

Saturday afternoon, Woollahra, Sydney

The face that greeted me at the door still had the same open, shining smile. The body, though, had less bounce. I thought I detected a slight limp as I followed her through the living room and into the kitchen where she introduced me to her husband, Alan Coles, and her sister, Margie. Alan offered me a cup of tea while Pat made arrangements to meet her sister later in the day.

'Great house,' I said to Alan. It's always safe to begin conversation in Sydney with real estate. It's a Sydney obsession. The real estate section in the local paper is really the social pages. That's where you find out whether people's fortunes are going up or down, and if so called 'celebrity' couples are splitting up only to cleave with others. No detail is spared. Even what happens to the family dog, if it's part of the settlement. It's brutal. As a convict colony, Sydney's culture was based on rum, sodomy and the lash. They've simply added real estate.

'We're selling,' said Alan. 'Pat wants to live in a pole house among the trees in Hunters Hill.'

'I do,' she said, intently. 'It's time for a change.'

My Adelaide upbringing (free settlers, no convicts, nonconformist) prevents me from including the details of our discussion of the estimated value of this house but I have learned to play the game. It's like Monopoly. You only deal in millions or parts there of.

Spying the mismatched cup and saucer that Alan had placed in front of me, Pat interrupted our calculations. 'Alan, could you possibly get Susan a saucer that matches her cup?' She rolled her eyes at me.

'I really don't care.'

'But I do,' she said firmly.

'Sure,' said Alan, and calmly replaced the saucer with one that matched.

The exchange, though it amused me, was totally without acrimony. Just a familial tussle between a couple who know each other's eccentricities and have learned to accommodate them.

I slipped instinctively into analysis mode. 'Mismatching things make your bottom itch, does it, Pat?'

'Yes, Susie. I'm very anal. Shall we move to the dining-room table?'
Clever girl, Pat. Doesn't miss a trick.

It took me years and years to realise that I didn't have to prove myself any more. All of my life I have felt like an outsider. From the moment I took up this job as a magistrate I was subjected to all sorts of pressure, particularly from police and the rednecks out there in the community. I had to be very, very tough. But it was only about two years ago in fact, that suddenly it hit me: 'I've actually got there and nobody can touch me.' Now it's as if I walk around in this little capsule or bubble. I'm immune from the slings and arrows. Part of it is being married to Alan. Not the marriage so much, but the influence of that personality on me because he is such a confident person.

We'd been married for a few years when it was obvious to me that everything in his life had bolstered his self-esteem and who he is in the world and his importance in the scheme of things. He was very bright at school, he took out the school prizes, all of his teachers thought he was the boy with the halo. Now I didn't have that experience in life. I had to actually prove I was a human being first of all, but it's been taken for granted that not only is he a human being but he's actually a super human being and he's somebody who deserves all these accolades for really just doing what comes naturally. One reason I married him is that he's an intellectual. He challenges me in a quiet, non-aggressive, non-confrontationist way, which is probably the perfect foil for me. At the same time he's got this total confidence in his own intellect and other abilities and he's not afraid. For years and years after we were married, I used to think of Alan as a god and then I realised I was every bit his equal and I thought, Wow. All these people all over the world, literally, who speak about him in such glowing terms, and here I am, every bit as good as he is. He was an academic in human movement studies, physiology, phys ed. We've been married for just over fourteen years.

He was a head of department at the same time as me. I met him within the first couple of months of my job. I went off to do a residential school for departmental heads. I used to trip over his long legs every time we had a break because he sprawled out. I stopped and spoke to him this particular day and invited him to have coffee with me. We used to just go and have lunch together. I did say to my secretary, 'One day I'm going to marry that man', and she thought that was hilarious. I certainly meant it. But the first time we went to lunch all he did was talk about his previous relationship breaking down and I thought, Oh God, not another lame duck, because I'd had enough of men with their lame duck behaviour and I wasn't going to be pulling anybody else out of their own garbage. But he's a very charming person. I scream at him, or I used to when I was very ill, and he would just seem to sail through it. He never ever shouted back, but he looks after me. He is intelligent, he's got an interest in world affairs every day, he's got an interest in the arts and he is very culturally sensitive. He's got a quiet and confident manner about him and he's very handsome.

I'm Chancellor of the University of New England, he comes with me. As far as I'm concerned he's got everything. He's a cordon bleu cook. He's not sexist. He is very supportive of me. Really, day in and day out, he's the only person I ever want to be with. Just to know that I'm going to come home to him, that's all I need in life. I don't even need to come home to my daughters. They live somewhere else anyway because they're both in their thirties. I need to see them but they're both overseas right now and having good fun with each other, I'm sure. But he's the person I really need to have in my life. It's given me a lot of confidence because he's got a lot of confidence in me. When his son was killed in an accident I was very good for him. Although he'd been through two relationship break-ups, that was the most serious crisis, to lose a child. I used to say to him that he was allowed to grieve, he was allowed to cry, and he would probably never get over it, and not to feel that he should get over it. I would allow him the space to feel like that.

The last time you talked to me about my life, I was about to be head of the Department of Aboriginal Affairs here in New South Wales. I think I am the only person who's ever been appointed a head of department in this country, anywhere in this country, and I would suggest anywhere in the Westminster world, in fact, who was not provided with any accommodation of any sort. I did not have one square inch of my own space. There was no office for me to sit in, there was no chair for me to sit on. There was not a piece of paper for me to write on, there was not a pen for me to write with. I mean absolutely nothing. On the first morning I sat in the minister's office in Parliament House—obviously that wasn't going to last too long. After all the media interviews, he suggested that I sit in a corner of his office, and I said that was inappropriate. The building manager was called up and he couldn't find anything. Funny how they can't find things when they don't want to. So I went looking myself.

The department was an abstract, it was a notion in somebody's head, and I had to do the lot from scratch. In that very first week I actually did find some space, in the Goodsell building, and kicked out some guy who worked for the bicentenary celebrations. When I went into his spacious office, which took up all of one side of the building, I found deep cabinets full of crystal glasses and loads of drinks and literally nothing else. I said, 'Oh well, we'll take this space', and the building manager told me I couldn't do that because it belonged to this fellow. And I said, 'Oh yes, and who else?' There were no staff there, and he said it belonged to the man and I said, 'Well, too bad, now it belongs to us.' So I moved in.

I had to set about finding myself a receptionist because the telephone calls were coming in left, right and centre, as you would expect. There had been quite a lot of publicity about my appointment and I was having to do all of that and my own correspondence. The Public Service Board after a few days allocated somebody to me who was seconded from somewhere else. He lasted a day and a half. So they allocated another fellow to me, who helped me to set up everything. He was an absolute gem, just a young fellow and very open and friendly. He and I got on exceedingly well and we were a very good team. Just before Christmas we needed some stationery supplies and he went over to the government printers in Ultimo and asked for them and they said to him, 'Oh, you'll need a requisition slip, they're known as C17As.' And he said, 'Well, how do I get those?' And they said, 'Well they come in blocks.' And he said, 'But how do I get them?' And they said to him, 'Oh well, you need a C17A.' He'd been running around in this shocking weather—it was very, very hot, lots of traffic—and he didn't get back to the office until about two hours after I expected him. He was red in the face and he wasn't quite sure whether to tell me because he thought I would explode. I just lay back and laughed. I guffawed. I said, 'When I write my memoirs, that's what it's going to be called— *C17A*.' I could not believe their stupidity.

I had to break rules, bend rules and throw them out the window, just to get started. It was absolutely no walk in a rose garden. Anyway, I can look back on that and say, well, that was a major achievement for me. The minister wanted to appoint me for seven years. I only wanted it for three years because I knew it was going to be a no-win situation for me. And so after three weeks we actually compromised on five years and at the end of that time I think we'd done pretty well. It's now known as the Department of Aboriginal Affairs, it's still going. I'm certainly proud of the work that we did. We had some very good successes.

I went to the magistracy from there. The magistracy is a fabulous job. In some ways it's my best job. It doesn't have the same challenges as the other jobs because you get into a routine and actually you're dealing with the same kinds of matters all the time, and yet the nuances or the variations of human nature are endlessly fascinating. And at the same time as I say that, sometimes you'll just get a stream of people, say on drink-driving charges, who will tell you exactly the same thing in exactly the same order of words. It's as if they all just looked at the script pinned to the courtroom door before they walked in. That is mind-blowing at times. You get it in those regular kinds of things, like assaults, for example, between young fellows who got into drunken brawls in pubs, 'But it was me mate. I didn't mean to hurt him.' That kind of stuff.

What I really love about this job is that I win every single day, without fail. I win. One is truly autonomous in this job. Nobody in the world can tell you how to do your job. Nobody. The Chief Magistrate has extra duties by legislation and he can direct us where to work, but he doesn't direct us *how* to work. The police in particular, in my opinion, waged a very long campaign against me. They didn't want me there, because of my ideology and my philosophies. I know what kind of language they used about me on occasions. Basically they thought I was 'agin police' and I was going to be giving in to all the crims. They thought I was a dangerous person to have on the bench. They couldn't do deals with me. Let's face it, over centuries the magistracy in particular, but the judiciary generally, has been corrupt in terms of its very close connection with other forms of institutional power. Nobody can do deals with me, in fact. They used to run these campaigns via talkback radio. There were times when I'd go to barristers and get legal advice because some of it amounted, in my view, to criminal libel. My barristers would say to me that it's pretty hard to go through with something like that. But I sued 2KY and the Police Association of New South Wales for defamation a few years ago and I won very handsomely. It took three years from the time that I actually took out the action. Basically they were saying I was not fit to do the job and that had always been their line, and there were racial slurs scarcely disguised. They finally settled but I wouldn't settle until I had an apology that had to be read out in open court. The world's media was there and it was everywhere by lunchtime that day. That was the third day of the hearing. My solicitors had said to me, 'Would you be prepared to settle?' I said, 'The money is nice but I want this apology and I want it stated in open court. I don't want this hushed up.' I wanted them to eat crow.

I didn't find any support from the other magistrates at all. They'd been congenial and in fact the magistracy has really changed in the time that I have been on the bench. We now have a very professional magistracy, probably the best magistracy in the English-speaking world. We're very highly trained. All of our people are highly qualified lawyers.

I got the flu when we were travelling in Europe and unfortunately I continued to travel at a time when I think I should have actually been in bed. I did go to bed for quite a while but I was anxious about our time going so I pushed myself and then I ended up being very ill indeed. I've had operations on my arms and my right hip and my left knee. Basically I've had soft tissue injuries but it was from the muscles going into spasm. I've had a lot of pain. It was all definitely stress, without a doubt. Some mornings I wake up and I can scarcely move, it's just terrible. I try to get in a walk every day but sometimes my knee swells up and gets so painful and my hip is painful, and I think, Oh my God, I won't be able to walk by the end of this week. I get through it. I had to have a lot of relaxation therapy because I literally had pain from head to toe, it was just really so bad. I take it very easy in the morning now. Once upon a time we'd have been on our bikes, into the gym, do a workout there, race back on our bikes, or down to the beach and have a swim. I don't think I'll ever have that kind of mobility again, unfortunately. I was very fit and feeling great until all of this illness hit me and it really struck me with a vengeance.

We don't wear robes in our courts, just your business suit, skirt and jacket or pants and jacket. We sit till four o'clock and have an hour for lunch. I always try to go for a walk during my breaks, morning tea and lunchtime. I need it because I've been sitting for a long time at the bench and when I stand up, very often I can scarcely move. I don't go to the common room with my colleagues during breaks because I need to have that exercise.

Walking along the street, people will recognise me and they'll stop and chat with me and ask after my nephew Tjandamarra. He's the youngest child of my youngest brother. Alan was overseas at the time and my daughter Marilyn was living here. I could hear the phone ringing. Marilyn was ill and I didn't want her to be disturbed by it so I raced in and it was my middle brother telling me that a man had thrown petrol on Tjandamarra and set him alight. I just started screaming, I just couldn't believe it. We went up there to see him and I have to say I have never seen anything like it. How that kid is alive today is quite beyond me. But what was interesting through all of that was this huge outpouring of sheer love and support from our fellow Australians. It was just the most phenomenal thing at a time when all of Australia was going through the whole Hanson thing and Howard was going on with his anti-Aboriginal stuff. It was ugly politics and then this happened and a huge tidal wave of love just swept over us. People flocked to the hospital with food for the family, gifts for the family. Money came in envelopes with no names attached, cards and letters. It took us all by surprise. It was very difficult to deal with because it was just constant.

A lot of people thought the attack on Tjandamarra was racially motivated. It wasn't, it was truly random. I'm pretty sure that he would not have lived if we all hadn't had that kind of support and if the family hadn't been able to draw strength themselves. We all believe that he was aware of us even though he was unconscious and in isolation and he was in a terrible, terrible way. He's fine now. He's coming along very well. He was very badly injured, literally from head to toe, and he has to go back to hospital every few months. What that did for me personally was drag up resources I didn't know I had. My daughters, my niece and I sat around this table that first night and we were crying and saying to each other, how could anyone do this? Because he was such a beautiful child. So for a couple of hours or more we sat here and we just were numb with the pain of it. The pain was here in my chest, a real physical pain. At first you don't know how you're going to cope with it.

There were phone calls backwards and forwards from Cairns and my youngest brother actually ended up going home by himself. I rang my oldest brother and said, 'You've got to go and be with him, we can't leave him in Cairns. He's got to be in Brisbane with Jenny and

Tjandamarra.' My daughters and my niece were here as well. I said, 'Don't you worry, I'll organise that.' I rang Ansett and explained to them what the problem was, that he had to be on the first plane out. The people at Ansett were fantastic. Everyone was, in fact. It was almost as if we were all hit by the same thought at the same time. We just said, okay, we've got to be strong, what do we do? The whole family's got to stick together. We've all got to be there and give him all the strength we can and pour all of our love into him. From being totally numb and in pain and crying, we suddenly changed and realised we had to be right there, stand strong and firm and summon up all the love to pour into him. That's what we did.

The Aboriginal community of Brisbane were just there with pots and pots of food and flowers and offers to take the kids and to do all kinds of things. But it was just the most phenomenal response you could ever imagine, from black and white people. That's when I realised that actually, when it all comes down to it, there is in fact a lot of love around and we need to be harnessing that all the time.

It's just terrible, the negativity and the hatred and the hostility that have been preached towards your fellow citizen. I always knew Hanson would be defeated. I always said that to any media personality who would ring me up and talk with me about it, but I thought it would last a bit longer than it did. I just couldn't believe how quickly the wheels fell off the wagon. Her own party deserted.

I took up tailoring classes because I realised that I had to get some better balance back into my life. I was sick of being sick and I needed to give myself recreation, and the best thing is to do something that's creative. I've always liked sewing and dressmaking. Right now I'm making an overcoat for my husband. I made an overcoat for my sister a few years ago and a very nice overcoat for my daughter. I've made suits for myself. When we were up there with Tjandamarra, holding that vigil, my sister was sitting there stitching and I'd be sitting there reading and my eyes would be going cross-eyed. There's only so much reading you can do, and I thought, I'll get into embroidery too. I'm glad I can do something creative because I've always thought that I'm not an artistic person. Actually I can do some very nice work with the needle.

The truth about my life? It's been a huge struggle. In some ways I don't know how to express it. I'm not good at stream-of-consciousness because I'm a control freak. I suppose for me the truth is that struggle brings rewards. But that sounds glib somehow.

I have got over all the hurt that I've experienced in my life but I've been through some pain, too, in recent times over that. In the last five years I really had to chuck it all out of my system. It's certainly very limiting. It's a waste of energy. I just worked it through myself. Since I had all that mental illness I've always believed that I have the strength now to get myself through any crisis. I don't fall into a heap any more. I've got that strength. I know the territory so it doesn't frighten me. Getting rid of it was certainly a release. You just get over it.

The Constitutional Convention was a farce. The power elite really gelled together to make sure that the ordinary people at that convention, and for that matter the great majority of Australians, were not going to get their way. They will maintain power at any cost and they are so deceitful about what a republican form of government means in this country. It means a fundamental change of the style of government, and none of that has been put to the people and the people have just been kept in the dark. They realised that if they voted 'yes' they were done, and if they voted 'no' they were done. Their option of democratic election just wasn't being put up there. The way in which Jones and Sinclair, who were the joint chairmen, let the likes of Bruce Ruxton be so rude to the women in that convention was pig stuff. It was disgusting. The only people who really got upset about it were Moira Rayner and myself, and of course we were known as 'the sibilant sisters'. We just started hissing Ruxton and his offsider, Garland. In the Resolutions Committee, Gareth Evans would just stand over us. Malcolm Turnbull thumped his hand on the table one day and said he wasn't going to put up with something and poor Moira, she walked out almost in tears. One day I said to Barry Jones 'I'm not going to stand for this, you're the chairperson. You'd better pull people into line.'

Over the incident with Malcolm Turnbull I said, 'I demand an apology.' Barry Jones said, 'I'm the chair of this committee, Pat.' And I said, 'Well, then you demand an apology.' I said, 'He's got no right to behave like this towards anybody else in this committee.' I said, 'Who is he?' If I looked like a harridan on television I can assure you I had a very good basis to be that way. You asked me earlier if I ever felt like writing my book, the story about myself. I don't, but that is one experience I want to write about. Otherwise the real story of what went on there will never be told.

I have more confidence now about expressing my views. When I did the Berlei Bra billboard case, my comments went around the world. It was one of those accidents in life because I had been rostered to work in the city and on that morning I'd received a phone call asking me to go to Balmain because the magistrate from there was ill that day. As soon as I arrived, I could see it was 'list day' because there were hundreds of people outside. I got into court and it was jam-packed with people and of course everybody in the world wants to be first cab off the rank. They want to plead guilty and get out of the place, or have their matter set down for hearing and get away as fast as they can. Just before morning tea I announced I was going to take a break, and this solicitor stood up. She was representing three of the women and this guy was representing the fourth woman, and it was malicious damage. I said, 'Okay, just hand up the papers. It's a plea of guilty, I'll deal with it and I'll read the papers through and read the facts sheet at morning-tea time and I'll let you know after that.'

I saw the photographs of the offending billboard, which was of this woman being sawn in half, and the slogan on it was 'You'll always be comfortable in a Berlei bra', and these women had added graffiti 'Even when you're being—' murdered or something, I can't remember what it said, but something to that effect. It was at a time when we'd been hearing a lot about violence. I was dealing with it every day. It was after that judge in Victoria had let off that guy on the basis that 'no sometimes means yes'. So when I got this case I just thought, This is the living end. I did find them guilty of the offence. There's no question about it, they did it and they said they did it. So I accepted their plea and found the events proved and I let them off on a 556A.

None of them had been before the courts before. They were all good, middle-class women, university students. One was a university lecturer, in fact. Then I sat back and launched into a bit of a spiel about violence against women in this society and how it just goes on all day, every day, and how this billboard was more of it, and how that was the real crime, to put that portrayal of violence up there. But of course these women had to face this property offence because it's a patriarchal society and they make the rules, and property law is more important than people's safety and so forth. Well, I got a rousing applause from everybody in the courtroom, which embarrassed me actually. I wasn't saying it for their sake.

Anyway, those women left and about a week or two later when I was just sitting here at home, a journalist rang me and said he'd heard about this case. At first I didn't know what he was talking about. And I said, 'Which case are you talking about?' He said, 'The one at Balmain', and I'm thinking, Balmain? I haven't done a case at Balmain. It was the last thing on my mind. He reminded me. I said, 'I don't have anything to say about it. It's over and done with.' But it appeared in the paper the next day. The phone started ringing at seven o'clock in the morning and of course it was on all the radio stations. All hell let loose.

Then I got invitations from universities and so forth to talk about some of those issues and some of the male law students in Melbourne ran a really savage article in the Melbourne Uni students' paper about my decision, attacking me. But they exposed themselves to be quite ignorant of the law, because I had actually dismissed the charges. The statement that I made was in fact made afterwards, it was not part of my decision. And in fact when the talkback radio rednecks got going, they said the Crown should appeal. They couldn't appeal because my speech was not the basis of my decision.

There was such a ground swell of public opinion over those issues. I'd be stopped on street corners. I'd just be standing ready to cross the street, men would come up to me. More men came up to me than women, but women from all over the world wrote to me, rang me up and said, 'Good on you, tell us more.' The Chief Magistrate's office was deluged. The Chief Magistrate said to me, 'Pat, tell them not to send their faxes to us, we can't handle them.' There were thousands of them and they came for years afterwards. Even now some people will still speak to me on the street about that decision. It was 1991 but it made lasting impact on people. One woman wrote to me and said that she had already written to Berlei to withdraw their ad, how she was going to boycott them and how she was getting her friends to boycott them. And within moments there were women all over the country saying they were going to boycott Berlei products and the advertisement was removed in three weeks. They were all removed.

I don't care whether they're male or female. It just happened that the case that I dealt with was female and they most often are female rather than male. But because an advertisement is demeaning to a male does not make it any better. It does not make it acceptable, which was the view that I think nobody expected from a feminist. I was invited to speak at business clubs for men and women, students, teachers, lawyers, the whole bloody lot. I realised that actually I'm in a position where people will actually listen to and respect my point of view. They take me seriously as somebody who can in fact influence change in this community. They realise that I'm not a one-dimensional person, I don't just focus on Aboriginal issues. I actually do have a point of view about all sorts of issues. That's just given me a whole lot of confidence.

I have a Masters degree in law and I've now been working in law for a long time. I used to think about Michael Kirby's statements from the bench. If he is prepared to say those things, so can I. For instance I'd come across police who quite obviously had lied and I would just say straightaway, 'You have lied.' I have referred matters to the

Attorney-General and to the police minister for investigation. People understand that I'm prepared to take a stand on some issues and I'm not going to compromise my values. What's there to prove now? I'm 58. I've got all this experience and it's been worthwhile. I know I'm strong and I know I'm capable and I know I've done it.

I am planning to do my PhD. It'll be on Aboriginal politics in the twentieth century. I really believe that some documentation of Aboriginal political movements in this century has to be done from an Aboriginal perspective. This is something that's going to earn me 'minus' brownie points. There's too much mythology about Aboriginal politics in this country and it's all very blokesy stuff. It's about blokes promoting blokes. Like Charles Perkins, for instance, who I think was promoted beyond his capabilities, and I'll say this straight out. In the years that he was with the Commonwealth Public Service, in various senior positions in Aboriginal Affairs, he achieved nothing like what I achieved in five short years with the state government in New South Wales. That's the up and down of it. And yet he is spoken of as though he is the father of Aboriginal Affairs in this country and it's simply a fantasy, it's a myth.

One of the other myths is this issue of nationhood, Aboriginal nationhood. It is the failure of men, first of all, to build from a grass-roots level. They don't have an ideology. If anything, they have the politics of opposition, whatever the issue. It does not have a philo-sophical and ideological core to it, and for that reason it doesn't have direction. The person who exemplifies that more than any other would have to be Noel Pearson. He came from North Queensland, from Hope Vale Mission. He's related to us tribally on my grandmother's side. All appearances were that he was a young Turk but I don't think he even made it to that grade, to be honest with you. His entire outlook on life is in fact white Anglo-Australian with a very strong undertone of German Lutheran, because after all that's where he was brought up. He's very clever with the words, very clever with the media, excellent at rhetoric. But in my opinion it has no substance. I don't attack the man, I attack his ideas. There is no recognition that we need to raise the level of intellectual discourse in this country. I think it's all very superficial and very much aimed at the five-second TV grab. Many people think Pearson doesn't speak for the blacks. I've had those complaints from people for years, ever since he first came on the scene.

I still question authority. I still have bite. Too right I have. I'm going to go to my grave with that. The more I've thought about my father in recent years, I recognise how much courage he had as well. I look back on the North Queensland that I grew up in and I think about how it must have been for him, a white man married to a black woman. I know how humiliated he must have felt on occasions when men would make remarks to him about his black wife. People are very ugly at times.

I still believe that education is the way to break the poverty cycle, even more so now from where I sit. The majority of people that we see in the courts are uneducated or under-educated, and certainly unemployed. School was paramount in my parents' book, and it's paid off. But then we get people like media stars saying, I didn't have an education, look at me, I'm a multi-millionaire, who needs an education? There's been a lot of that under this conservative wave that has swept the country in recent years, since 1996.

Alan says that other women, as well as men, feel intimidated by me, and I don't understand it. I don't think I intimidate other women. Of course I'm strong. I know that men can't cope with me because I am strong and I will not take any nonsense and I'm not about to fall about being a simpering little wimp. I think I've conquered myself in terms of my psychology, always feeling an outsider and not feeling confident about my abilities. That part of me I've conquered and got over. Anyhow, insiders don't do much because they're too comfortable. It's always going to stay with me, there's no question about it. But it's not something which spurs me to prove myself again and again.

When other girls of my age were getting very excited about having sex, I used to wonder what all the excitement was about. Sure I had crushes on guys when I was a kid but it was never a drive. I remember one girl in particular that I went through high school with, sex was everything to her and I used to look at her on Monday morning and she'd go right off about who she'd been with on the Saturday night. I even knew some of the guys and I used to wonder what she was getting so excited about. I don't think I'm completely asexual but it's a very low sex drive. I have a strong love drive, but that's a different thing altogether. Sex has nothing to do with love. It's just another urge, a bit like a need to eat or a need to drink. I put it at that level. I'm more romantic than Alan. It doesn't have anything to do with sex. It is to do with loving him. I actually think the romance side of it is more exciting and titillating than the actual consummation.

My emotions are not as intense as they used to be. I get pretty angry still over injustice. I think some of that energy has gone and left me through illness, through literally being totally fatigued.

I just wish women would get their bloody act together and get going again. For years I've been saying to them, midnight on 31 December 2000, women are going to take over the world. I see inroads being made all the time by governments into all of these gains that we made through the seventies and early eighties. At first they were being chiselled away by Hawke and Keating governments, and now of course Howard can just sweep them away. He's absolutely blasted some of them away. And where was the reaction? There just wasn't any. I have contact with young women only through my daughters. They're two very strong women. I don't know how to get to the women who are representative of the masses of women. The vice-chancellor and myself are two very strong role models and we're right there at the top of the administration of the university. But women are losing ground everywhere. The tide is definitely out. If Hillary baby made it to the White House, I reckon we'd see a resurgence. I think she must be a pretty tough lady.

I have not seen a woman or women make an appreciable difference to the way in which boards operate. For instance, corporations and banks. If anything, they operate even worse than they did before. What do these women do when they get there? The world hasn't changed, has it? If anything it has actually gotten worse. I mean, what have they done in terms of maintaining women's rates of pay, for example? The pay differentials are slipping. More women than ever are engaged in part-time work.

What's the answer? Get on your bloody horse, Lady Godiva, and ride all over the top of them. Why do you want me to answer these hard questions? I think a new wave is going to come very soon after the new millennium dawns. I really do still think that. Where did it come from in the late sixties and seventies? The human species has to learn to live and cohabit with all other species in the world and I think that's going to be the big crisis, the environment. That's where women will take control. That's where women will come into their own again.

I do think femocrats let the side down. I said a long time ago in Canberra that we had a responsibility to ensure that we did open doors for other women, and a lot of women didn't do that. Once they got there, that was it. They were just like the men, and in fact they started to adopt the same attitudes. I was at a conference and I said this, and boy oh boy did I cop it. Wherever I have been, I've tried to use my position to open the door for others or to encourage others to open the doors that they find in front of them, and there are ways you can do it very effectively. It doesn't take any effort and truly it doesn't diminish you at all. What used to worry me was that a lot of femocrats fell into the male power paradigm and it really bugs me. They became very bureaucratised.

I worked in the Department of Women's Affairs, the Office of the Status of Women. The attitudes of some of the senior women to the very junior women in the place horrified me. They treated them like slaves or handmaidens. They'd be horrified to hear me say it but I did say it to them all the time. We should be using power as a liberating force. That doesn't mean when you're power sharing that you have seven women sit down around this table and discuss how we're going to make that decision or a decision in respect of that issue. What we say is, we've got a number of issues here and we all can't deal with them, therefore we'll share the responsibility. You do that and I'll do that and you'll do that. It's that kind of leadership and decision-making that's lacking. We have to seize that momentum. Now.

health farm

*P*at O'Shane has stopped trying to prove anything to anyone. Even herself. She no longer gets stressed by forcing herself to do things, just to prove herself.

It's time I did the same.

There's a part of me that would really like to thumb her nose at women's continual and obsessive attempts to achieve the perfect body. Even if the rhetoric is all about health, I still suspect that deep down it's really about appearance. The seemingly endless desire to be thought attractive, to be thought acceptable. Who is proving what, and to whom?

In the 1970s it was all 'my body, myself' or 'fat is a feminist issue' and we were determined to learn to love ourselves, whatever our shapes. In the 1980s it was Naomi Wolf in The Beauty Myth, *saying it all over again for another generation.*

And yet the 1990s saw the same parading and lauding of anorexic bodies in the fashion pages and in the sitcoms. Women spent an even larger part of their lives dieting, going to the gym, having a personal trainer and generally obsessing about the size and shape of their bodies. They always claimed it was for health reasons—but get a group of women in a room together and they'll start talking about losing weight or hating the size of their stomachs or their behinds. It is as though Naomi Wolf never existed. My favourite television programmes were 'Two Fat Ladies' and anything Dawn French was in, particularly 'Absolutely Fabulous' and 'The Vicar of Dibley'. Here were women who clearly didn't give a damn, who cheerfully thumbed their noses at the prevailing 'thin industry' and were happy just being who they were.

And yet I still found myself going to a health farm.

I'm not fit. I'm overweight. I'm sluggish. I'm totally undisciplined. How could I possibly begin to write a new book? Healthy minds come from healthy bodies. Perhaps I should go to a health farm? Somewhere like Cape Fear in Queensland. That should cure me of sleep, sloth and an addiction to carbohydrates. Good idea. But don't those places charge like wounded bulls? It will be worth it. Put it on one of your credit cards and pay it off after the book is a huge success. That's what you say about everything, that's why you spend so much time doing journalism, giving speeches and doing fill-in broadcasting. It's always to pay off the bloody credit cards. And they keep getting bigger. And bigger.

Writers are meant to be poor and struggling. It's good for them. And anyway, what would you do if you just did nothing and stayed in Sydney? Go out to lunch and talk about how you can't get started on the novel. You'd have a drink and go home and have an afternoon snooze. Now they call it a power nap. What a joke.

This new century is so full of spin. No one has a life any more, they have a 'lifestyle'. The thirtysomething women are always complaining about how tired they are. No baby boomer would be caught dead admitting they were tired from overwork. Pleasure, yes, but never drudgery. And why do they work such long hours? So they can have a lifestyle like the ones in *Cleo*, *Marie Claire* and *Vogue Living*. All the right labels on their backs, the designer body, the designer home, the designer dinners, the designer partner, the designer holidays. Those that can't have it, lust after it. There is no joy, no madness, no wild leaps of the imagination.

'Getting and spending we lay waste our powers.'

So why are you spending money you don't have to go to a health farm?

Because I want to be at my peak to write this book. Sure it's not just another delay tactic? Better sleep on it.

All my friends agreed I should take the plunge and go to Cape Fear. I didn't think I was that overweight and unfit, but it seems they have all been worried about my propensity for denial. Denial? That's nonsense.

I had one small croissant on the plane. Could be my last taste of real food for a week, I thought.

A limo met us on arrival. Thank god. Thought they might make us walk half the way carrying our luggage. Just to get us in the mood. We pulled up at a high green timber gate. The driver plucked a phone from a cavity in the wall and announced the names of his occupants. Slowly a giant gate slid away. We glided through. It closed automatically behind us. Trapped. Strange, how much you pay to be locked up. Golden palms lined the drive and we curved to a stop outside a small building marked 'Office'. A tall, tanned, twentysomething ran or rather bounced up to greet us, jumped into the limo and instructed the driver to take us to the chalets. Where were we? Switzerland?

A simple country motel room is how I would describe the plain but clean room that confronted me. Pink chairs. Turquoise carpet. Narrow beds. Australian bush prints on the walls. There was, of course, no television and no radio. We had all been asked to surrender our mobile phones. I had handed mine over, smiling, docile. Lobotomised.

Why, suddenly, did I have this feeling of dread spreading through my body? Was it too late to escape? Could I feign illness?

I'd done it before.

Once when I was a very junior lecturer at a teacher's college, I had volunteered to chaperone a group of students on an excursion to a place called Innamincka. Don't ask me where it is. I had never heard of it but the lecturer who talked me into it convinced me it would be a fascinating insight into the mid-north of the country, where I had never been. An adventure. I thought, Why not? As the bus pulled away from the campus I'd had this same feeling of dread. The rising panic came later.

After a day spent singing jolly songs on the bus, a night spent singing even jollier songs around the campfire, being awoken by a student screaming that there were rats in her tent, being given a shovel to take to my early morning ablutions, I knew I had made a terrible mistake. A truly terrible mistake. I also knew that if I didn't do something to get out of it—that day the bus would take us into the desert, from which there was no escape.

I had to act.

A degree in literature gives you many things, one of which is the knowledge that there is no plot that cannot be reversed. I had been reading Heller's novel *Catch 22*. What would the main character, Yossarian, have done in such a situation? He would have lied his way out of it. All it needed was imagination. After breakfast, when the students were packing up the tents, I took my fellow chaperone aside, and with an expression bordering on the tragic told him in hushed tones why I could not continue on this excursion. I knew that if I mentioned words like 'blood' and 'flooding' he would not want to press me for details. I was right. He went pale. He nodded wisely. He said he understood. He agreed that the best solution was to stop at the next town, where I could get a plane or hitch a lift back to the city. I impressed on him the urgency of my problem. He had visions of menstrual blood spilling, spurting, onto his new white sneakers. He couldn't wait to get rid of me.

The college bus pulled up outside the hotel that was the hub of activity of the nearest tiny town. I stared at my shoes and looked solemn as my colleague explained to the students that unfortunately I had to return to the city urgently and that he was very sorry I would not be able to share this wonderful experience with them. I waved goodbye as the bus disappeared in a cloud of red dust, and even though it was only ten in the morning, I raced into the bar for a gin and tonic to celebrate my good fortune. I was elated. I felt like I had won the Christmas raffle.

It took me twenty hours to get home, having cadged a lift with a truck driver and his mate. They insisted on stopping at every pub on the way. I sat between them and it was a full-time job keeping one awake and the other from touching me up. But it was worth it.

I couldn't get away with the same ruse here, though. Mention flooding and they'd just give me Maxipads and organise a stricter diet and exercise regime. I couldn't send myself a telegram. I couldn't ring anyone for help. I had to face it. I was trapped.

The first form they gave me to fill out was a straightforward assessment of my health, past and present. The second form, however, was concerned with more intimate revelations.

DO YOU FIND IT HARD TO CONCENTRATE? Only when I have a book to write.

DO YOU EVER GET DEPRESSED? Only when my credit card payments are due.

DO YOU BECOME IMPATIENT AND AGGRESSIVE? Only when I'm asked stupid questions.

DO YOU DRINK ALCOHOL TO MAKE YOURSELF FEEL BETTER? Is there any other reason?

DO YOU GET WHAT YOU WANT OUT OF LIFE? Not until I win the lottery.

Please spare me from all this soul-searching banality.

The third form was a real ripper. You had to tick one of the following

N: not at all.

O: occasional.

F: frequent.

C: constant.

I managed to deal with headaches, allergies, colds etc. but baulked at 'spitting up phlegm, bed wetting and pus in urine'!

Where was I, the intensive care ward? After this we were given our name tags. I should have chosen a more exotic name. At least I could have had some fun fabricating my life story. Madonna Michelli had a nice ring to it. Two massages and a facial were included in your package but I signed up immediately for a 'stressbuster massage, a pedispa, an eye-zone wrap and a bronze sensation'. All for only an extra $150.

At the completion of my fitness assessment, I could hardly lift myself up off the floor. The consultant said in a tone she no doubt thought sympathetic, 'Never mind, dear, we all lose muscle strength as we get older.'

Older! How dare she.

I opted immediately for a personal trainer. Only $280 for four one-hour sessions. Was this the price of privacy or vanity?

Lunch was served in a large timber-framed building with mock colonial furniture. It was a buffet. You could choose from broccoli, green salad and something beige in a paste form. I suspected chick peas had lived there once. I sat at the end of the table and ceremoniously dropped my bag on the chair next to me. Well, it was better than slapping the first person who talked to me.

How, oh how, did I let myself get talked into these things? All that money. How many lunches could I have indulged in? Why did I con myself into doing things that were supposed to be good for me? It always made me feral. This was like a Sunday school camp. But I couldn't ring my mum and dad to come and save me. Might as well just throw up my hands and go under.

As long as no one talked to me. Or worse still, smiled at me. Why did they have to all be so cheerful? Some of these people would smile in solitary confinement.

The afternoon was spent in the gym with Shane, my personal trainer. Shane was patient and, thankfully, the silent type. Or perhaps it was just my body language. I spent the rest of the time in the loo. You were expected to drink five bottles of water a day. You got your own bottle with your name on it. They kept count. Amazing they didn't make you keep the pee. Had a competition.

'Now all hold up your bottles. The one with the most urine gets a free massage.'

I skipped volleyball. Lying on my bed, I searched in vain for a way out. I stared at the timber ceiling, counting the boards over and over again, as if they held some pattern yet to be discovered. I stayed there thinking, fully clothed, my sneakers tightly laced, for what seemed hours. When I finally emerged distraught, the woman in the parachute-silk designer tracksuit, with a face to match, called out brightly, 'Coming to dinner, Susan?'

Food. They were going to feed us.

Dinner was the same as lunch. Only hot.

There were a few middle-aged men with big guts, a few couples who continually joked and laughed as if we were all on 'Candid Camera' and a large number of exceedingly thin young women who certainly did not need to lose weight. After camomile tea, when I was tempted to eat the teabag, I removed myself from the pleasure of their company and returned to bed.

At 6 am there was a good morning tap at the door and I leapt out of bed fully clothed.

Once assembled outside, we were paired off. Fortunately I got silent Shane. We were told to give each other a neck and shoulder rub. Followed by a bum pummelling. Poor Shane must have thought he had landed in a tub of suet pudding.

Tai chi was at least a hands-free activity. Gentle. Tranquil. Ethereal.

Inside I was raging. I hated this emphasis on the body. I realised I always had. All of my life I had actually pretended that I was somehow invisible. Easy to do when you are young and you are not too fat or too thin and have the kind of body that is unremarkable. Only when I was fourteen and self-obsessed did I spend hours looking at myself in the mirror. My father caught me and said, 'You'd be better off concentrating on your mind, young lady. You don't have to worry about your body. It's fine.'

So I didn't worry.

Until now. And now, it clearly wasn't all right. It felt as rusty as my dad's old Holden. About to fall apart. I resented even having to think about it. Was I finally having my mid-life crisis? Was my addiction to lollies and pastries the result of a deep-seated depression? I decided I should be in analysis, not paralysis. Five minutes into the walk up the hill and I seriously thought I might have a heart attack. At least it would have got me out of there. The idea of the cool white sheets on the ambulance trolley seemed like heaven. However, it was a somewhat drastic way of escaping all this agony. I puffed on. Nothing happened. I plodded on.

And on. And on.

Breakfast, when I was finally able to breathe, was fresh fruit. I chose to eschew the sensual pleasure of the porridge when I saw someone standing their spoon upright in it, like quick cement. The morning was spent with Nathan the naturopath, whose main concern was teaching us when and how food entered and exited the colon.

I have to admit that I did not previously know that at 9 pm my breakfast is waiting in the sigmoid colon, still waiting to be expelled. Lunch is mainly in the transverse colon and dinner is ready to enter the colon. Is my life richer for this knowledge?

Perhaps I was just missing my morning coffee. Cappuccino, latte, espresso. I promised never to take them for granted again. The only good news was that red wine is better for you than white.

Oh for a beaker full of the warm South
Full of the true, the blushful Hippocrene
With beaded bubbles winking at the brim
And purple-stained mouth.

I was close to dribbling. But Nathan was focused on flatulence. He said that with this kind of diet and massage, it was important to not hold back. There was a lot of schoolyard giggling when he seriously asked us to give the staff fair warning before we let one rip. Oh please! I had come all this way and paid all this money just to enter a farting marathon. No wonder they needed aromatherapy.

Finally a facial, followed by an eyewrap. I fought hard to stay awake long enough to stagger back to the chalet.

I managed to shower or at least slump upright and let the water run over me. I felt like Janet Leigh in *Psycho* after she'd been stabbed.

Lunch was baked pumpkin and bean salad. I sat at the end of the table. All those beans were very dangerous.

The rest of the week went by in a blaze of beans and a blur of body bumping.

I lost two kilos.

I thanked everyone profusely.

I declared that I had turned my life around.

As soon as I reached the airport I ran, stumbling, to the nearest machine, bought a Violet Crumble bar and stuffed it, whole, into my mouth.

Oh the joy, the joy of that chocolate-coated golden honeycomb.

The truth is that unless you really want to change, no amount of persuasion or rational coercion will work. We are creatures of emotion and I had failed to be saved. Perhaps I was beyond redemption. My Sunday school had encountered a similar problem. Heathen to the end, I was enough to make any evangelist weep.

When I got home I hated people telling me that I looked great. A false tan can work wonders. But it was all false. I was no different.

Flatulence can take you only so far.

The visit to the health farm had been a farce. Not on their part but on mine. Why did I continue to con myself into believing that by forcing myself to go I would be forced to change my behaviour? The truth is that whenever someone tells me something is 'good' for me, or that I should do it, I resist. Stubbornly.

Perhaps the unpalatable truth, a truth as hard for me to digest as the breakfast muesli, is that I am perverse. Incurably so. And secretly, that's just how I like it.

What was I trying to prove to myself by going to the health farm?

I know that if I really wanted to lose weight and get fit, I could. I clearly don't really care enough but pretend to myself that I do. Or perhaps I just want to hand over the responsibility to someone else.

I had failed to make the most of what was being offered at the health farm because I wilfully refused to become part of the ruling ideology, the communal whole.

Just as I had refused to lead the life that my aunts had kept telling me was my fate. Just as I had refused to be part of what was expected of girls. Just as I had refused to be part of the team of women whose main role in life was to be that of male helper. I did not want to be the tugboat which guides; I wanted to be the ocean liner which cuts its own path through the sea.

When I was five years old:

I knew that the only time my male cousins accepted me on their cricket team was when there were absolutely no other boys around.

I knew that being on the team did not make me one of the team.

I knew it didn't matter how well I played, I would be dropped as soon as a boy was available.

I knew it wasn't fair.

But it didn't stop me trying to beat them.

Photo: Greg Barrett

MAGGIE TABBERER

Fashion designer, marketing consultant

Youngest daughter of a poor family, three sisters and one brother, spent her childhood in Adelaide. Bored with school, she left at fourteen and had jobs with a pharmacy, a hairdresser's and an accounting firm, all of which she hated. When she was seventeen she married a much older and more sophisticated man and had two daughters. Started modelling in Adelaide and moved to Melbourne, having been discovered by the famous photographer Helmut Newton. Finding her husband autocratic, and gaining some sense of independence from earning her own money, she stayed in Melbourne and he returned home to Adelaide without her or the children.

Now a very successful model in Melbourne, she moved to Sydney after falling in love with the man who was to be her second husband. Having put on weight, she moved into other areas of the fashion industry, design and promotion. As a panellist on the popular television show 'Beauty and the Beast', she presented her own programme, 'The Maggie Show', won two gold Logies and went on to write her own fashion column for the *Daily Mirror*. Her only son from her second marriage was a victim of cot death. She became fashion editor for the *Australian Women's Weekly*, launched the Maggie T clothing range for larger women, and her public relations business developed into Maggie Tabberer and Associates.

She relies on her intuition, her ability to organise, and her attention to detail.

She relies on her ability to surround herself with the best people, and her tendency to overcommit, to provide her momentum. She never looks back, is not introspective and is always ready for the next door to open.

Her apartment, Rushcutters Bay, Sydney

When you know someone as well as I know Maggie, there is no point in pretending to do a formal interview. From the very first time that I met her face to face and interviewed her, our friendship has grown and grown. Now I live not only in the same building, but opposite her. The doors to our apartments are open and we wander in and out of each other's domestic arrangements, each other's strengths and weaknesses and each other's fears and hopes and dreams. There's not a lot that we don't know about each other.

No two people could be more different. We are, as our mothers would have said, as alike as chalk and cheese. She is a doer, I am a thinker. She is neat and tidy to the point of being obsessive, I am happiest in a mess of books and newspapers. She always looks smart and glamorous, even if alone. I like nothing better than staying in my sloppiest clothes all day and only dressing up if I have to. She left school at fourteen, I have three degrees. She pays great attention to detail, I wouldn't notice if half the furniture disappeared. She is very much a homebody, I would be out every night if I could. She goes to great lengths to avoid conflict, I relish a good stoush. She is susceptible to flattery, I am instantly suspicious of it. And so the list goes on. However, and it is a big however, we each have great admiration for what the other has achieved and we spend a lot of time laughing at the same things.

In her apartment, after dinner and over a bottle or two of good red wine, we engaged in what could loosely be called a discussion of her life. I was her mentor, editor and friend when she was writing her auto-biography, and she became the basis for my theories on the power of praise that were to form the basis of my book Be Bold. *Needless to say, the role-playing was an outstanding success, as her book was a huge best-seller and she left behind the pain and the heartache of her last relationship.*

It's strange, isn't it, how you go in and out of certain people's lives, depending on their needs or yours. It's enough to make you a firm believer in Jung's theory of synchronicity. 'There you go again, another bloody theory. And who in the hell is Jung?' Maggie would say. 'You'd be better off putting on some make-up and throwing out those terrible pants.'

Pross, my second husband, and I eventually split up. He fell in love with someone else and it was very painful. I moved out of the house after a lot of argy bargy about whether I'd keep it or he'd keep it. Eventually I just said, 'You bloody keep it', and walked away. It was the right thing, in retrospect. Regrettably, what he thought was going to be the love of his life didn't turn out to be and they had a very short marriage. He went back to Italy and many years later died sadly and alone. He told me that he regretted that he broke us up, because even though we were living very separate lives there was an enormously deep, strong love between us. I had lots of affairs but I would never have made the move because I loved Pross and still do.

Before we split up I'd started having an affair and when we split I thought, That's it, I'm never going to live with another man again. I'd got myself a white house with white tiles and white couches and white walls, and said, I'm never going to have to wipe shaving cream off the mirror again or pick up dirty socks. Eight months later my lover left his wife and came to live with me and we were together for ten years. About five of those were excruciatingly happy and then gradually the rot set in. I found him trying. He was very selfish and he was absolutely useless around the house. It never occurred to me to ask him why he wouldn't clean up. I simply sold the white house and bought one in Hampton Avenue, Darling Point, more perhaps the sort of house that he really liked. It's the only house I've bought that I've hated. There's a lesson in there because I bought it to please someone else, not to please myself.

Ultimately I was the one that still had to run it and maintain it and do everything. Two flights of stairs to press a shirt. It was a hard house to operate and I was really glad to sell it. But I sold it and bought a farmhouse called Borey Bills, which was lovely. He'd lived in the country and I thought he might miss it. Also, I'd had the boat for several years and while I loved it, I thought he was more country. Idiotic, isn't it? I can't say that I didn't love the farm. It was a cruel twist in a sense because I then became absolutely passionate about Borey Bills and then went on to become more passionate about Greenville, the next house, than him. It ultimately made both our lives very happy and I adored it.

We did the 'Home Show' together for four years. I really didn't want to go back to television. I thought I was old and I didn't necessarily want to go through that grind of 'What are you going to wear and how many changes and is your hair all right?'

I'm not an idiot about all things but I'm certainly an idiot about men. If I fall in love, I fall really deeply in love and all I think about is, is my partner happy? What would be fulfilling for him? What would give him great joy? I think I do that and thousands of other women do that. It's part of the joy of life. Giving is as rewarding as receiving. He bought a little house in Paddington and we moved into that as our town house, after we bought Greenville in the Southern Highlands and moved down there. The days we filmed, we needed somewhere in town.

I helped him do his house up and then we decided that he needed a better investment and I found this marvellous old twenties apartment and really went to town on that and did that up. We moved in there for a while and we were still living at Greenville, and then I said to him it was too much of a luxury and he could get a really great rent for that and be paying off his mortgage. So I said, I'll just buy us a little place. He wanted to go to Bondi because he liked to swim each morning. So I bought the place in Bondi. Ho hum, fiddly dum. I sound like a dolt. I am a dolt. I see the pattern, of course I see it. It's disgusting. I hated Bondi. The rubbish, the itinerant people that would just go away and leave old dirty mattresses on the street or bloody old refrigerators on the street and throw their papers or bottles or milk cans or soft-drink bottles over the bloody front gate into the garden. So when we split, which was while we were there and still living at Greenville, I was very quick to sell it. And that's when I bought here, which was a really good buy.

I stayed on at Greenville. When he started to play up, he found excuses to be in town more and more and more, and I had a great sense of responsibility about Greenville but I was also passionate about it. I felt centred and I loved it. It was a great house to entertain in. People used to love to come and stay for the weekend. After we split I came to the slow realisation that I should move back into the city. If we had stayed together I'd still be there, definitely. It was a wonderful life and a wonderful house and gorgeous to be on the land and to see the seasons and it was very gentle. But it became very lonely and very uneconomical, me rattling around that great big house. And a great responsibility. There were staff in the cottage, there were animals on the property. I could go away to Italy for three weeks but I couldn't go away for three months, which now in my new life is what I want to do. I was absolutely determined I wouldn't sell until I'd found me again and centred me again. I went through all that great angst and anger and pain and hurt and that's when I started to write the book. I was committed to the autobiography and I felt Greenville was the best place to do it.

The wisest thing I've ever done is not marry again. I didn't think it was necessary at our age and I really didn't want to. He asked me to marry him many times. I used to tell him to go and have a glass of water and lie down and the urge would pass. I just knew that it wouldn't be right. There was nothing to gain from it and there could be quite a lot to lose. And as much as I loved Pross, and I'm sure he loved me, ultimately I didn't come out of that marriage with what I was financially due. And that had happened with my first husband too. There was a strong sense of survival and I'd worked too hard in the ensuing years. I can't say I ever really sat down and calculated, but unconsciously I'm sure it was there in my mind, 'No Maggie, don't do this, it's not a good move.' I toyed with the idea and thought it would be romantic to wear a caftan and stand under the oak tree in summer and get married and then I'd wake up the next morning and think, Are you mad?

He was outrageously jealous and it didn't stop at my family. It was close friends as well. I knew immediately that the distance between him and my daughter Amanda was very apparent when he literally snatched me out of her arms when she came home in the very early stages. He used to say he just wanted to see me by myself. He was completely open about it. It is flattering. But it was awfully difficult. My heart was torn. I'd think, My God, they're my children, I want them around. We muddled along and went to a psychiatrist who said, 'You've got to set boundaries. He lives at Greenville too and when the children come out, you can't have them there morning, noon and night. You give him a break so you have a few days with him and then you have the kids down.' I tried to manipulate that but it was bloody hard. One of the hardest things I've done was trying to keep everybody happy. But I always do that.

I wanted a totally monogamous relationship—because I had fooled around and Pross had fooled around, and I think you not only get to hate your partner, hate who he's with, but you hate yourself and who you're with. It's demeaning to your soul, to be living a life like that. When he and I fell in love, I said, 'If we're going to be together, this is how it's got to be. Don't ever cheat on me because you won't hear the click of the gate.' I always said it and I reiterated it all through our relationship. I guess I'd say it with humour. If he'd be going off to the races, I'd say, well, don't let a big-titted blonde race you off, but he knew that I meant it. Anyway, the big-titted blonde emerged. I caught him and that was that. As painful as it was, there was never ever a question of having him back. You feel betrayed and vulnerable. I was going through the menopause. That's a big enough battle without anything else buggering up your life. The age factor is a cruel twist. She was younger. I saw it happening and I was powerless to do anything about it. I thought that it was his mid-life crisis. I felt like I had wasted ten years of my life on this man. I had great joy with him for a number of years. Whether he got on with the kids or he didn't, or my friends liked him or didn't, it didn't matter.

He was so different from anybody else that I'd ever been with or had a long-term relationship with. I'd been with a European for 29 years and before that it was Charles, who was much older and more sophisticated, and suddenly here I was with this mad Aussie larrikin who wanted to go to the footy and talk about the races. And I loved it. I say constantly to various friends and my children, and I say to myself, nothing lasts forever. You want it to. Of course you do. You want it to be right, and I felt we were so lucky. I used to look at Greenville and our life. We lived in this amazing house, we had a nice apartment in town. We had jobs. You think to yourself, How can this not be enough?

My mother always tried to make everything right. She was illegitimate and when she got her own family she wanted everything to be right all the time. Of course the truth was far from that. My father was drinking himself into a stupor, they were battling for money. That's where that side of my character came from. You can't fix the world, but you know, I still try. I don't know why, I just want everything to be smooth. It's not just for me that I want everything to be right. I want it to be right for my children, I want it to be right for my friends.

I've seen a lot of people struggle to stay together and shore up, shore up. They break up and they go through all that agony and they come back together again and then they go through the whole bloody painful process again, and for me that's too hard. I think you're better doing a cut and run. On the other hand I have seen long, long marriages survive affairs and hurt. If I had been much younger I might have thought, I can rebuild this. But when we went into that relationship we were both very mature people. He was eight years younger but he was hardly a kid. I would never trust him again. I used to think about it when he rang and tried to come home, and I said, 'I will make both our lives hell because every time you drive out of that driveway to go to the races or go wherever you're going, I'd be sitting there thinking, Who he's with and what he is up to?' I don't want to get a mouth like a duck's bum. I look at women like that—I can name a half a dozen in this town that live with husbands who they know play up—they've all got mean, really tight little tense faces. I'd rather be sitting at home by myself, with my good mates coming by for a glass of wine, and not having that in my life, not going through that agony of worrying about a partner. It's terrible. It's awful. And they give off such unhappy vibes.

You always have choices. Charles felt that he could blackmail me into coming back into the relationship by threatening me that I wouldn't be able to survive and I wouldn't be able to look after the kids. He said, 'I'm not going to support the children,' thinking that that would be the thing that would send me scurrying back to Adelaide, because I'd be so fearful. It just made me more bloody determined to get it done. All the things that men admire about you when they come into the relationship—that you are strong, you are capable, you are independent—five years or ten years or in one instance 29 years down the track, suddenly they say you're too strong. There are a lot of women that will play-act, they'll do the little helpless thing. It gives me the shits.

I'm very proud of my book and its success. I'm stunned and proud. As an autobiography it's a story of survival. The mail has been amazing. So many women write and say, I saw so many parallels in my life. Of course, they'd say, I haven't led a glamorous life like you and I haven't travelled, and then they list the things that they see as parallels. They may have been through rejection from a partner or losing a child. A lot of women that have lost children to cot death wrote. A lot of people wrote about their early childhood. The surprising thing was the number of young women that wrote and said they'd felt inspired. They felt that I'd done so much in various careers. I'm thrilled if it inspired people to get off their bums and have a crack at something. I've had women write to me and say, I was so inspired I'm starting my own business, or I'm going to drop everything and I'm going to travel.

I wouldn't choose to come back as a man next time. I'd probably want to come back as another independent woman. The truth about being a human is that you have to at some point of time in your life, for me in particular, come to a realisation and an acceptance that it's not possible to control all facets of your life. You can do your damnedest and your hardest and you can work for it or manipulate for it or wish on the stars for it, but you have to, at some point in time, accept that you just can't control everything.

I would still wish that every woman knows the full roundness of life. That they would not be stuck out in the suburbs with five kids and never know what it is to have a fulfilling job and work satisfaction, whatever that means to them. Whether it's running the local fish and chip shop or running the tuckshop at school or making a living with Tupperware parties or running a corporation, I don't care. But I would like to think that there is a way for them to have that satisfaction and also still have a family. You can have it all, without running yourself ragged, or feeling guilty about it if it doesn't work out.

I love men. I like matching wits with them. I like being around them. I think they're good animals. I find women are more direct and they'll tell the truth, regardless of the consequences usually, whereas men don't necessarily lie, they just avoid the facts. There's some wonderful men, there's some mediocre ones and there's some bastards. Time has got nothing to do with it. Women have changed enormously but I don't think basically men have changed. What concerns them is power, money, position and power. I confess I'm quite enticed by power. I think it's sexy. Strangely, though, I've never had a relationship with a really powerful man. Anyway, I'm the last person in the world that you should ask to analyse men because obviously I don't know much about them. I'm not bloody good at choosing them. Not too many of them are brave enough to make the approach to me, which is the strange and curious thing.

Life's journey is still a sense of discovery. The only time you perhaps have a great moment of clarity is when you're about to cark it. I've tried to think deeply about it and I can't get a handle on it. One of the things I have got a handle on, which is so fascinating and intriguing and frightening and joyous at the same time, is coming to terms with aging. Not being old—I don't ever want to be old—but aging. There was a certain amount of time in my life where I could cheat with my appearance. Then I had all the emotional trauma of the last break-up and me not wanting him back and then the journey of the book and starting a new life. It took its toll. I see a lot of women who go under the knife and come out looking worse than they were before. I've consciously made the decision that that's not the way I want to go. But I'm at ease about it.

It's good to reach this age and be calm about it. Maybe it's not about being in your sixties and alone in the city and building a new life. Perhaps it is that suddenly I don't have to please men. Mind you, I have a couple of admirers that come calling and I always race around and try and make myself look good. I'm still not over that, but I'm talking about when you get out of the shower and you catch a look at yourself side-on in the mirror, and suddenly thinking, Well, this is where I am and I don't want to stuff up whatever's left of me in this life by being anxious and bitter and tense and racing off and having plastic surgery and putting me and my family and my loved ones through all of that terrible thing. You've got to welcome aging and there's a wonderful, new found tranquillity about saying: This is where I am and it's good. I've said I didn't want to live with another man, and I don't. That doesn't mean I wouldn't like an affair.

I just know that if I cock my leg out of bed between six and six-thirty and get on with the day, there's a salvation and a sense of achievement of living that day as fully as I possibly can. It's not my nature to be deep thinking and analytical about life. That might be the reason that when I tackle something I've never done before, I'm often successful at it, because where angels fear to tread, I'll go. There's a balance in life. You have to know that some things you're going to do very well and some things you're going to do very badly. My defence is that I've never picked bad men, they've picked me.

There's a sort of burden in being considered beautiful because you think, No one's going to give me the same flexibility as they'll give their sister or their auntie or their cousin or their mum to get older and not be so beautiful. I really want to cast that off. I'd like to just think people thought I was a beautiful lady but not necessarily in the way that they termed me before. I do get embarrassed talking about it.

I think I'm a good mother. I don't think I'm a brilliant mother. I would have liked to have spent more time with them and closely monitored their education, but there wasn't an option. I was the sole breadwinner. I moved into a very public profile and I regret that my daughters feel they've had to share me with Australia. And it's sad, in a sense, that they did. Everybody wants a piece. But I did my best.

I think I've gotten a bit lazy about being a lover. But I'm a generous lover. I'm a very good friend. I'm passionate about my friends, my inner circle. I was a pretty terrible daughter. When I was young I caused my family a lot of pain, had an abortion, got married at seventeen and my husband left me with two kids. I was probably a worry to my mother. I'm glad she lived long enough to see me have some measure of success and think that I wasn't going to be a total dickhead. I'm generous in business. Too generous actually. I'm a good wife. If you're talking about wifely things, like running houses efficiently and looking after my man and cooking and cleaning and doing all that, I'm excellent. It wasn't done begrudgingly, I enjoyed it. I loved being efficient at all that and running it well.

I don't ever want to be with a man who's got another relationship in train. I don't want to risk causing another woman that sort of pain.

But you know what I really like? I like having my own things. I liked being in Greenville. I liked making it beautiful. I liked the sense of achievement and owning a property that looked like that. I like the sense of achievement of now having turned two apartments into one. It's spectacular. I look at it and I think, It's mine and I did this, and I love that sense. So it's hard, I would think, for a man to slot into that.

I like sex with the whole bonbon. I just don't want to get on the bed and go hump, hump, hump. I want all the game-play that goes with it. I have to feel something for the person. They either have to woo me or there has to be that sort of chemistry. I want the glass of champagne and beautiful music and the beautiful place where it's going to happen. Romance is the thing.

In business I've often felt on the back foot. I've had to go out and get legal advice that's cost me a lot of money and I've resented it because it's been really because I was a woman. I pay people to get experts in the field. I think it's intelligent to know where your abilities are and to absolutely capitalise on them to the maximum and then know when, outside of that, you're going to need help.

I'm not a fighter, I hate it. I hate confrontation. I am quite courageous about some things in life but I'm just not naturally aggressive. That's my mother's influence. Keep things nice, keep things calm. Walk around the corner rather than have a blue with someone. I do, however, regret that in some business instances I didn't make a stand.

After a long period of feeling very shaky, I feel centred. I feel a new surge of confidence. I don't think that I have to have any sort of partner. I love my friends and I love my family and I want them all to be in my life. If passion came along tomorrow I'd absolutely love it, but it's not the beginning and end of my life. It's not the criteria for me feeling fulfilled any more.

christmas day

Maggie has spent a lifetime trying to please her husbands, her lovers, her children, her employers. She has always tried to create a perfect world. In order to achieve this she has taken control because then she knows it will be done properly. Perfectly.

She has moved from state to state, bought and sold houses, decorated and redecorated, lived in the city and the country, juggled, balanced, walked the tightrope of conflicting demands—all in order to please. Mostly men. In so doing she has often ended up pleasing nobody and being accused of being a 'control freak'. Christmas, for example, she always planned and plotted down to the last minute detail. Women are always in charge of major events in the family and Christmas, the biggest day in the calendar, usually creates the greatest amount of stress and misery for those responsible for making it a happy day. For Maggie it was like a military manoeuvre. Nothing was left to chance. Everyone was to arrive on time, to wear white, to sit in their place at the long beautifully decorated table so that the day would progress with everything timed to gourmet perfection and precision. Maggie made sure nothing ever went wrong.

Like everything else in our lives, my experience of planning Christmas day had been very different from hers.

But even I have tried, in my own fashion, to do my best to create the kind of Christmas Day that was expected of me. Women still spend their lives trying to please others and trying to do everything perfectly.

Why we do this? Why are we always trying so hard to please and to be perfect? At what stage in our lives do we decide to please ourselves and give up perfectionism? This was the day I gave up even trying.

One Christmas I spent in a bus.

I had been overcome with the desire to live in the Hills, those misty bosoms of romance. And daffodils. It was spring when this urge found its voice. Well versed in my many dramatic phases, my father suggested I rent a place before taking out my next mortgage. Nestled in those soft green cushions embroidered in blossom was the cottage where I knew I would begin to write.

The voice that answered the ad I had placed in the local paper said it was a perfect retreat.

'It's a cottage?'

'Not exactly.'

'It's not cream brick, is it? I wanted something well . . . special.'

'Exactly . . . but you'll have to see it for yourself.'

And that was how I came to be standing next to the giant trunk of the maple tree that spread its branches over a rather strangely shaped, elongated fibro shack. It was Christmas morning and I was waiting for the old white Holden bearing my mother and father to turn into the drive. I loved them both, but Christmas was never easy. I was no longer sheltered by the enthusiasms of childhood and large family gatherings. Our small group of three seemed more aware of its fragility with every passing Christmas.

I'd hoped the day would be pleasant enough to eat outside. I'd pictured the three of us under the maple tree, sitting around the red and green tablecloth, wading through the traditional three courses. But the day was as grey and hot and lifeless as the dead bird I had nearly stepped on that morning. Not a leaf was stirring. Not even a mouse. Bushfires flickered in my nostrils and my imagination.

We would have to eat inside, where my ancient fan would roll its stale breath from side to side. No doubt the original owners had enjoyed many a jolly Christmas lunch, there in the fibro dining room they had attached to the double-decker bus that overlooked two valleys.

The main body of the bus served as the living room. Two bunks, a settee and a couple of chairs were squeezed in the space where once the seats had been ranked. The circular iron staircase, up which the conductor had rattled his coin bag to the top deck, now led to the bedroom. A mattress on the floor, walls lined with books and windows that at night shed enough light from the moon to silhouette the pine trees as they swayed with sudden gusts from the gullies—this was, I believed, a writer's dream. Somehow, though, I hadn't managed to write a word.

There was the car now, winding its snail-like way, down the treacherous drive. Father was as always first out of the car. He strode towards me, the discomfort of his suit and tie apparent in his gait.

'Happy Christmas, my girl.'

'You didn't have to wear a coat and tie, Dad. It's far too hot.'

'Your mother insisted. And, well, it is Christmas after all.'

When we kissed I felt the perspiration lining his upper lip.

'Could somebody please help me,' came a shrill call from the car.

Having safely negotiated mother and her walking stick from the car to the airless asbestos box, I wondered if the faint throb over my left eyebrow would develop into a migraine.

'Here's cheers,' toasted Father, draining the flute of champagne in one swallow.

'Happy Christmas,' said Mother, her pearls glued into her neck like shells in sand.

Presents were opened. As usual there were few surprises. We kissed and smiled. Even smiling seemed to increase the temperature, which was not mentioned. I should have booked a table at an air-conditioned restaurant instead of allowing my fantasy of the day to rule.

'Never thought I'd be having Christmas dinner in a bloody bus,' snorted Father, skolling another glass of champagne.

'You'd better keep the wireless on in case of bushfires. I don't know how we'd ever get out of here,' said Mother, little crusts of make-up outlining her frown.

Moving to the window, Father swivelled his head as if to detect the first wisps of smoke. 'We'd be trapped if it came up the ridge. No point in taking to the scrub. Too many snakes on a day like today. Hard to know what to do, really.'

The pulse in my head quickened. Silence settled itself around us like a second blanket of heat.

'Let's have the first course. Dad, you help Mother to the table. I'll carry the fan and put it near her.'

It was while I was pouring the pink sauce over the curled bodies of prawns half buried in strands of lettuce that I remembered an old bottle of Valium someone had given me for times of crisis. Unsure of whether the drops falling onto the seafood cocktails were sweat or tears, I was sure that what was rising in my throat was panic, the kind of panic reserved for celebrations with my parents. Why did I always believe it would get easier? I rummaged through the kitchen drawers with such ferocity that Mother called out, 'Anything we can do to help, dear?' Not sure of their age or strength, I popped two tablets in my mouth and took a swig of warm champagne.

The heat from the oven slapped me hard as I dragged out the roast turkey and three vegetables. Father removed his suit coat and loosened his tie. Mother dabbed at her forehead with a lace handkerchief and fanned herself with a Christmas card, even though her face was inches away from the fan, which was fixed in her direction.

Carrying the turkey and its trimmings to the table, I was aware of a strange lethargy that had begun to spread through my body. The large white platter thumped onto the table, making the salt and pepper tip over. Mother threw the salt over her left shoulder. For luck.

'Always found turkey a bit on the dry side, myself,' said Father, drowning his plate with gravy. And dry it was. So, too, my mouth, which seemed to be having difficulty getting its tongue around words. The clicking of dentures and buzzing of the fan created a stereo effect inside my head. I had another glass of champagne. So did Father.

'What's next?' he said, loosening his belt.

'Christmas pudding, of course,' said Mother.

Wondering how I could get my legs to move, I heard myself singing, very slowly, 'Immortal, invisible, God only wise.'

'Are you feeling well, dear?' said Mother, patting my hands, which were clammy and closed on my lap. 'Let your father help you with the dishes.'

'I'm fine,' I said. Little rivulets of sweat trickled down my back as I dragged myself to the kitchen.

Staring down at the pudding bouncing around in the boiling water, I wondered what it would be like to plunge my hand into the saucepan. I should have taken only one of those tablets.

'Don't forget the brandy sauce, dear.'

Oh shit, the brandy sauce. Brandy would have to do. Pulling the steaming, gooey mess out of its cotton cloth, I dropped half of it on the floor. Knowing if I bent down I might never get up, I formed what remained into a mound by cupping it in my hands.

I poured on the heated brandy and struck a match. 'Tirrah,' I slurred, lifting the plate with great uncertainty and turning towards the dining room, where they were seated with their backs to me. The flaming brandy licked the nylon curtains hanging over the kitchen sink and a strip of flames leapt up the fibro wall. Transfixed by the speed of the flames as they spread higher and higher and the black flecks of nylon landing on the pudding, I knew I should do something but couldn't think what. I dropped the plate.

Father came towards me in slow motion and began to beat the wall with the sole of his shoe. First one shoe then the other. The flames flickered and disappeared.

'What on earth's happening?' called Mother, unable to turn without difficulty.

'Nothing to worry about. Just a spider,' said Father, stepping back in his socks into what remained of the pudding.

'I can smell burning,' Mother insisted.

'A little accident with the pudding, that's all,' he said, winking at me.

'How about a beer, me girl? A nice cold beer will do us the world of good.'

'I'd like a cup of tea if there's to be no pudding,' shouted Mother. 'It's not really Christmas without a pudding,' I heard her mumble.

Later on, much later on, when they had each taken to a bunk for a little nap, I dreamed of charred legs, turkey legs like Mother's. I was stuck up to my neck in a huge plum pudding, unable to speak because of a sixpence in my throat.

I awoke, wet through, with a furry tongue and a clear head. Underneath the rhythm of their snoring I heard the faint but distant roll of thunder. Rain was not far away.

EVE MAHLAB

Businesswoman, company director,
consultant

Only child. When she was two her parents fled Vienna to Australia, to escape Nazi persecution of Jews. Earliest memories are feelings of fear and apprehension. Always had tremendous feeling of opposition to oppression. Her parents manufactured dolls during the war, in sheds behind their house in Melbourne. As both parents worked, she became very independent at a young age. Very close to her father but often in conflict with her mother. A social outcast at school. Teachers considered her a troublemaker. Very bright student but not allowed to attend speech night because she had told a teacher off.

Her father always told her she would become a lawyer because she was very difficult, very outspoken, and very independent. He also wanted her to regain their lost status and position. She tried hard to please them and graduated in law. Married a businessman and had three children in three and a half years. Hated being stuck at home and knew it was bad for the children. Started a very successful agency for part-time lawyers, joined the Women's Electoral Lobby and became very involved with the women's movement. A tough fighter for change within the system, for women to have more choices. On the surface, she always led a conventional middle-class life.

Cocktail bar, Rushcutters Bay, Sydney

She was in Sydney for a board meeting. We agreed to meet for a drink. Short, attractive, with a generous smile, she was wearing what was undoubtedly a very expensive suit and looking suitably corporate. She would hate that label, 'Corporate Woman'. She has never fitted any label and yet in a way she doesn't really understand why she never fits in to the organisations she is involved with.

There in the fading light, as the trees, the park and the water gradually dissolved and then disappeared into the darkness, she drank her pina colada. Only the one—as opposed to my two gin and tonics—because she doesn't really drink much. I could not imagine her ever deciding to let loose and become legless. Her form of rebellion is more intellectual.

She talked admiringly about corporate women who really knew how to play the role, women who remembered the names of the blokes' wives and children and asked how they were doing at school, where they went for their last holidays, what their favourite sport was, which football team they barracked for.

'But you could do this if you wanted to,' I challenged her.

'No. I couldn't. I simply can't remember.'

'You don't want to remember. You're really not interested.'

'That's true.'

'Anyway, it's just a form of schmoozing up to them. You wouldn't schmooze up to anyone.'

'No. I think these women are genuinely interested. You can't remember all that if you aren't.'

'Most people use personal information to impress powerful people.'

She didn't look convinced.

She is naive in some ways. Many of these women would memorise a mechanics manual if it would help them climb further up the greasy corporate pole. She lives totally in her own head, so much so that she is incapable of placing herself in someone else's shoes. She does not lack sympathy, but sometimes lacks empathy. These are entirely different qualities.

Over dinner she asked me quite genuinely, as if it had just occurred to her, 'Have I taken too much mashed potato?'

As if it isn't obvious that you have taken too much when your plate is piled high and there's nothing much left! The time to ask, as any mother training a child would say, is before you take your own share. What could I say? 'Yes, you have, as a matter of fact', and get her to scrape some off her plate and onto mine? I didn't want any more potato but if I had said I did, she would not have been offended. Only children, particularly those who spend much of their childhood in isolation, take as their reality only what affects them. Sometimes it's as if other people simply do not exist, except as vehicles to exchange ideas. Sharing, community, playing with the team—these are concepts that in practice are unfamiliar to them.

I called a taxi to take her to the airport and stood waiting to wave her goodbye. She was not looking. She was too busy giving instructions to the driver. I waited and waved until the taxi disappeared around the corner. But she never looked up. Or back.

I still have enormous anxieties. And fear. I don't know of what. It's a floating anxiety. I usually tell Frank, my husband, and he tells me, don't be silly, or it just passes. I do try not to make big decisions while in that state. I still want to fight every battle but I've learned that perhaps you can be strategic and just choose your targets and issues. I'm not fighting men any more. I now think they're just as exploited as women. It's such a complicated issue, but fifteen years ago, perhaps I didn't realise it. Some men have the power and the others are as marginalised and as exploited as a lot of women. Women now have much more access to public power. Today the issue is not whether you're a man or a woman so much as whether you're a parent or not. It's being a parent that makes the difference. If you've got responsibilities for a child or an elderly parent, that's a real disadvantage in the public arena, whether it's work or politics, because you've got these competing pulls on you.

I had the sort of mind that made the compromises almost auto-matically, so they didn't feel like compromises. Today men and women both make those compromises. In retrospect, men compromised their closeness, their intimacy with children, for advancement. They were as much confined into those roles as we were into being wives and mothers. It was just as hard for them to break out of those roles as it was for us. There are still elements of it in organisations and it is still harder for women to be in the 'in' group. But it's very hard for a lot of men to be in the 'in' group too. A lot of men are precluded because it's a case of cronyism. The men who advance are cronies or clones. People pick people like themselves. When women get to managerial positions, they tend to choose women. They first of all choose women because women, they believe, do the job better, and they communi-cate better with the women, and the men don't do things in the way that they'd like to see them done.

I constantly feel like an outsider. I consciously go to places where I am an outsider. It may be a learned thing, it may be a strategic thing, subconsciously. I don't know why. I guess it's almost a positioning thing. When I was maybe seven, eight, I used to play the piano accor-dion. I never liked playing the piano accordion. My parents wanted me to play it, and I also went to ballet school. But I played the piano accordion very badly and I danced very badly as well. So when they used to have the end-of-year concerts, the music school always had me dance and the dance school always had me play the piano accor-dion. I didn't know why then, but I knew that I was different. I wasn't like everyone else. And I think perhaps I learned something from that, that there is a benefit to being different. I actually add something of greater value to the group in the way of diversity, and they appreciate that and I get something in return, which is probably appreciation and I suppose success. You still feel an outsider but you see that there are advantages in it and it really doesn't upset you that much. One of the benefits of getting older is that you don't need to belong any more. I'm a niche. If you're a niche, there's no one else there.

I can't make polite conversation or smalltalk. It does worry me.

I would like to be able to do it. I watch other women who can. I know that's what you're supposed to do and I can't do it to save my life. Very often people pair up with people who represent what's lacking in themselves. Frank enjoys chatting to people. The truth is, I need time out. I'm certainly not a social outcast. I feel successful. I feel socially acceptable. I feel I'm a worthwhile person. I don't have any problems with that.

I ask a lot of questions and that irritates a lot of people, men in particular. I cannot control the questioning, the outspokenness. I've tried to. It works for a short time, but I blow it. It creeps in. I'm not a team player, I'm not a groupie. I have to say that it means you're seen as not predictable, not safe, so it really interferes with achievement in a way. I think particularly in business and in organisations you need to be 'one of us'. Your loyalty has to be counted on, and I don't think people generally feel that they can count on me.

'Making it' really lies in the eyes of the beholder. I'm on one major board, Westpac. I haven't been invited onto any other major board. The word probably got around. One of the things that happened shortly after I joined Westpac was there was a client lunch at a club that didn't admit women. I discussed it with the chairman and said that I would prefer not to go. He and the managing director were both shocked and they developed a policy of Westpac not having any more lunches at clubs that discriminated against anyone. Since then Westpac has had its board functions at hotels. But you do pay a price for taking that sort of action. If I did it again, I probably would be more strategic, perhaps worked on it over time. I was probably short-sighted. It had the right effect in one small place, but I thought that if I made that as an example, other women board members on other boards would follow suit and the clubs would be hurt in their pockets and be forced to admit women. But they didn't follow suit. Did it surprise me? No, I guess it was more a hope than a conviction that they would follow suit. The same imperatives apply for women as with men. They want to get on in the corporations or in the organisations and they're probably more sensible than me. In retrospect there would have been better ways of achieving what I wanted to achieve. I'm too impulsive.

I still like Frank a lot but at my age it's not a great physical buzz. When I was young I was more worried that more men weren't attracted to me. At that time men didn't want independent, outspoken women. We've been married forty years. I still find him attractive. I enjoy his company. He's a *mensch*, a human being, it's a Jewish word. And he has enormous self-esteem. He anchors me. I have this theory, and I don't know whether it's appropriate because it's not particularly thought out, but women fear getting out of control and they often look to men to keep them in control. Frank doesn't keep me in control in an imposing way, but he anchors me. I think I could have stayed at work 24 hours a day, wanted to be on 50 000 different committees, would have accepted every invitation to be on every association. He'd always say to me, 'What do you need this for?' And then I'd start thinking, What *do* I need this for? I do have a lot of opportunities but I say no to a lot of things, and I watch some other women and they say yes to everything but I'm not sure they get the satisfaction. I cherry-pick.

If he was having an affair, I think I would hope that I wouldn't find out. I don't want to know. I don't think it would have broken up the marriage. It might have undermined the relationship somewhat and left me with some anger. I have had no reason to believe that it was happening. I considered having an affair once but didn't go through with it. I actually gave it a lot of thought and decided I was risking too much in my relationship with Frank and it wasn't worth it.

Perhaps I'm not highly sexed. It's just never been very important. Not even when I was a teenager. Even romance is pretty boring. In the women's movement some women I know left husbands who were okay, looking for a thrill, and I think they sacrificed something that was very valuable. They could have been involved with the women's movement, as I was, and gone through all that and still sustained the relationship with their man, whoever it was. They could have worked on changing the man. I was never tempted with other women. It doesn't appeal. Do you think it's possible that if you're highly sexual you want to have a bash either way, because you're curious about sex?

I'm not a sensual person, but I'm a loving person. Oh, wait a minute, am I a loving person? No, I don't think I'm even a particularly loving person. I'd like to be a loving person. I think I'm too solitary for that, actually. I'm fairly self-absorbed and I don't think most of the people who know me would describe me as a loving person, and my children would just think that I'm fairly thoughtless, that I'm a dutiful person. If they point out what's the right thing to do, I'll do it, but I never think of it.

There was not a lot of hugging. I scratched their backs. My daughter gives her little boy a massage at night when she puts him down to bed and he loves that. I'm more physical with my grandchildren because I feel I should have been more so with my children. I do miss the cuddles myself. I do like that physical, affectionate thing that children give you. I was not good as a mother. I certainly loved my children but I didn't have good mothering so I didn't have anyone to learn it from. Now there are lots of books on it but there weren't when I was having them. I thought that if you moulded your children, if you sent them to the right schools and gave them the right advice and manipulated them the right way, that they would be happy adults. And that's nonsense. If I compare myself to my daughter and her husband, they regard their children as almost flowers that have to unfold. Everything is there already and all they have to do is nurture it and love it and listen to it. There's none of this moulding that I thought we had to do to be dutiful parents.

As a lover, I don't know. I'm a good friend in the sense that if someone needs me and tells me they need me, I'm there for them, but I'm highly unlikely to notice that they need me unless they pull my attention to it. Frank is a bit of a loner too, so we've got two loners living together and giving each other space but being there for each other. As a daughter? You'd have to ask my mother. She'd probably say terrible because I wasn't the sort of daughter she wanted. She's still alive and living in Melbourne. As a partner, it depends what perspective you have. If you're looking at the traditional perspective of someone who cooks, not very good. If you're looking at it from the perspective of a 'thought' partner, then very good. An emotional 'thought' partner. He's still there with me. He's told me that he's happy.

Becoming Qantas Businesswoman of the Year was the beginning of a really bad few years. Isn't there an old saying that the worst thing that can happen is that you get what you want? It made almost all my relationships in business reassess their relationship with me. Suppliers charged me higher fees, I had to pay higher royalties to the Law Society, my business partners felt put-out. It was very good in that it reinforced my credibility and gave me lots of kudos. I was getting pretty bored with what I was doing. It was really a micro business and I didn't have the ability to build it to a definite stage where you could professionally manage it. Key people left and set up in competition. I was due to go to Nairobi for the Women's Conference in 1980 and my recruitment consultant told me the night before that she was leaving and going to set up in competition. So I didn't go. I had to get on the road and get different staff. I was good at start-ups. I wasn't good at building them beyond a certain stage.

With every business you need a certain infrastructure and basically you can get a certain amount of profit but you have to grow it to get beyond a certain stage. In 1987 I could see that there was a major recession coming. I had received offers for the business, particularly the recruitment business, and at that time businesses were changing hands for fifteen times their earnings, ridiculous sums. So I sold. I kept the publishing side of the business and I invited Karen, my daughter, to come in and then asked her if she would like to take it over. She did and I moved out. That was really difficult because she didn't want me giving her advice and she's successfully built that up into her own business. I always thought that she would take it over but she'd be coming to me as an adviser, but she didn't want that. She wanted me away. I can understand that now but at the time I was deeply hurt.

There was a stage when the children were leaving home, either going to university or overseas. Even the dog died. It was a fallow time. I made a film with Ann Deveson. She was the producer, I was the executive producer. I raised money for it. It was on women and leadership, on SBS. I thought that would be a new career, that I'd make documentary films. But having made one, it was so difficult and it was like starting a new business with every film. I realised that wasn't the way to go. I was on various government boards, community boards, and having quite a lot of leisure at the same time. It was okay but I don't look back on that period as terribly productive. And not terribly interesting either. It was also a time when not only did the children move out . . . I don't know whether it's common but I think that children tend to reject their parents in their twenties. They really want to do their own thing.

Westpac wanted to be the employer of choice for women and I think that was one of the reasons I was invited on to the board. They always wanted to position themselves in small business. In my head there were changes going on. You start off thinking you can change the world, and as you get older you narrow your focus. Here was a corporation wanting to change by advancing women and I saw it as a micro opportunity. It was really interesting and a huge learning curve. I learned about organisations and how difficult it is to achieve change when working through other people. The minute I had to have a middle layer of management I found it enormously difficult, and at Westpac I could see through several layers of management. On the other hand I could see that in many cases the business objective got lost in a large organisation. Even now, not many people on boards have ever owned their own business, have had their own money on the line.

Men are basically team players. They love hierarchies and they're very protective of each other, have a lot of respect for each other. I'm not being dismissive or contemptuous of how they act. It's very easy to knock it. On the other hand, if you know that everyone is on your side and you're all focused on where you want to go, it may be effective. There's a lot of productive stuff that's happened that way. If you're a capable woman, you've got the same qualifications as men, an MBA, and you're in your mid-forties, and you can show that you're prepared to commit yourself to the group and the objectives of the organisation, I think you'll be welcomed. It doesn't advance the cause of women. The women who are successful on boards are only advancing the cause of women by showing how competent women can be.

I still think that small business is the way to go. If I had it all over again, I wouldn't change my career path at all. Women are probably closer to markets and they can see things better from the point of view of the customer and the consumer, and that's very important in starting a new business. But when it comes to building the business, to putting in the levels of management and taking the finance and doing the networking and relationship building with people outside the firm, I'm not sure there's much difference between men and women. If anything I think men may be better. After Westpac there's just been more boards, other boards. I don't think there's a lot of passion in my life for anything now, really. I play with starting another business. On the other hand, do I want to maintain another business and have to go in there every day? In a way I envy you. To be able to have skills that you carry around with you like a little house, like a tortoise with a house on their shoulder. If only I had something like that and I was passionate about it.

I think I have good ideas. I'm good at starting businesses. I'm not good at taking partners. I'm doing a consultancy at present for a Melbourne stockbroker. I'm good at problem solving. I'm good at seeing solutions. I'm not so sure I'm good at implementing them. I may be. I don't want to knock myself too much. I did build several profitable businesses. The other thing I did in those few years with a partner is start Carols in the Domain.

I satisfy my feminism in things like contributing money from time to time. I've taken wealth very much for granted. It's still an area of anxiety. I still assume that something terrible might happen. But there's part of me that knows I would survive. I am a survivor. I know that, but it doesn't stop me bearing it in mind. My need for money has been to get away from insecurity. It's not to become wealthy or to succeed in some way. I'll never have enough money to feel secure.

My sixtieth birthday party, where hundreds of women came to the St Kilda Town Hall as a fundraiser, was very satisfying to me. It was very good for my self-esteem because they were women who had some sort of connection with me or the women's movement. And it was fun. That was what I wanted. I wanted to dance, and I knew that if I had a party where we invited our couple friends, the men wouldn't dance. But I knew women would be out there dancing. I wanted it predominantly to be female because I knew we'd have more fun. When women get together it's almost as if you've taken the lid off a pot.

In the 1970s I had wanted to be preselected in the Liberal seat of Prahran. They had one of these 'meet the candidate' nights. One of the pre-selectors, who was an elderly woman, asked me, if I was successful, what would I do about the fact that 75 per cent of people in Singapore had had sex-change operations. I thought to myself, What am I doing here with these turkeys? Although I didn't use the word turkey in those days, I thought, This is the end, I'm not going to put up with this any more. I gave up all thought of politics after that. I said to her, 'I really don't think it's a state matter.'

In the 1990s I don't think I realised how bored I was on a day-to-day basis. I still found Westpac very interesting, was president of Philanthropy Australia, which is the umbrella body of the grant-giving foundations, the Myer Foundation, the Potter Foundation. The philanthropic movement is a bit like the women's movement, you're changing a culture and it involves legislative change and it involves public awareness. It's got all the elements of it, perhaps not quite the same passion, but nevertheless it's a bit of a mission and so that's quite interesting. There have been some successes there that I can see I've made a big contribution to.

But a few months ago, virtually at the beginning of the year, I was approached by a Melbourne stockbroking firm to do a consultancy for them on cultural issues, diversity, equal employment opportunity, and I took that on. It was hands-on problem solving. They offered me an office in the city. I share a personal assistant. It's only been a few months and it will come to an end, but it was only when I was hands-on again and working in an office environment that I actually realised what I'd been missing. When it comes to an end I'm going to have to find something else. I have ideas about Internet businesses. I don't know whether I'll ever do anything, because I'm a bit scared of getting tied up in something. I'm scared of the obligations.

The passion of the women's movement is missing, there's no doubt about that. Maybe you can only have one big passionate cause in your life. I think I was lucky to have one. Most issues relating to women are still the thing that turns me on most.

Opportunities in the workforce for women have absolutely increased enormously. On the other hand, for most women, incomes have gone down. In fact, looking back, I didn't realise it at the time but the real cause of the women's movement, or the real drive of the large-scale movement of women into the workforce, was falling male wages. From the end of the mid-1960s, really, household income was going down because of the end of the industrial era and men's wages were going down. In order to maintain the family, household incomes and household standards of living, women moved into the workforce. We still do not have equal pay but women are now locked into the workforce to maintain those standards of living in the same way that men were.

Capitalist society has really adapted or produced the whole shift. Women weren't forced into the workforce because of the women's movement. The women's movement actually demanded the benefits for them in the workforce, whether it was equal opportunity or conditions. But male and female conditions for the large majority have deteriorated in terms of security. Women are relatively better off now than they were then, but the majority of men have gone backwards as well. There are small numbers of both men and women, usually married to each other or in the same sort of class, that are doing brilliantly. I think probably the middle class have gotten poorer. I think the poor are probably either the same or even possibly a little better off. It's the middle classes who have suffered. Which is ironic because it was really the middle-class women who went into the workforce to maintain their living standards. We had to get our education, we had to get jobs so we could maintain the standards of our families.

Both my daughters have to work. They both have their own businesses. They both have partners who are very cooperative and helpful. My son is not married yet and has no partner, and it will be interesting to see what he chooses.

Whether they call themselves feminist or not, more women are on about equal opportunity but it's very individual. There is no collective approach like the one that we took. The collective angst is just not part of their agenda. They're fairly careful—they have to be, because they'll be stigmatised and punished in the corporate world if they're too assertive about women's issues, or radical. They know that and they're afraid of being typecast. Of course there are exceptions to all this.

I've had the best of both worlds. If I had the choice I think I'd be happy to come back as a woman. Even with the early trauma. The Austrian government is offering compensation to people who were expelled from the country, even to people like me, and you have to fill in this form. I was filling in the form and I thought, My goodness, I haven't really suffered like my parents did. I haven't suffered by being expelled. I've actually benefited from the whole thing.

Being Jewish used to mean a lot more to me. I still think that the Jewish people over 5000 years have made enormous contributions to society. I think Jews just do things very well. Even when they're crooks, they make a very good crook. But I think I used to equate being Jewish with being a minority. As I've grown older I see that the similarities between people are much greater than the differences.

There weren't many Jewish women in the women's movement. There were a lot of Catholic women. When I was very young I didn't even know I was Jewish. I don't believe in God. As I get older, I'm not coming back to it, I'm getting further away.

There was a period after we moved out of our family house, for two or three months, that I was very sad. I thought that a very important era in my life had finished and it was going to be downhill all the way. Nothing could have been further from the truth. I don't think I've reinvented myself much. I've responded to opportunities that have come up, and that has resulted I suppose in what looks like a reinvention but it's not been conscious.

When I see that women have been overlooked or forgotten or ignored I get absolutely enraged because there's no history of their achievements. As a Jewish person I realise how important knowing your history is, how important it is for your self-esteem. You can't go forward unless you know your past. The women's movement will be written out of history, it will be forgotten again. Do you know that the research for the contraceptive pill was funded by a woman? Her name was Katherine Dickson McCormick, and Margaret Sanger was a friend of hers and together they went to a scientist called Greg Pincus and he did the work. After I sold my business I wanted to make a twelve-part series on the history of women and I did the research. The ABC put $25 000 towards it, I put some money towards it and the BBC were very interested. But then the BBC went through all that restructuring and they lost interest. It just ended up with that one documentary, which rose out of the ashes. I think Ann Deveson did a fantastic job but it's not nearly on the scale that I could envisage. So I was very disappointed about that. We go two steps forward and one step back.

Frank and I used to talk, pre-women's movement, about how nice it would be to be passionate about something. We really envied people who were like that. And then the women's movement happened to me, not to Frank. So I was lucky.

I am sad when I think of different times when one or more of my children have rejected me for whatever reason. That's happened with each one of them at some time or another. And with my mother. My children and I get on extremely well now and each one of them I feel very close to. My relationship with my mother is still difficult.

I'm very easily bored. Ideas sustain me. Not any ideas but ideas about solutions, ideas that solve problems. Information technology is going to be huge. Even more so because it's about communication.

Women have never had a lot of money, and it's going to make communication much cheaper, and women will be able to talk to each other and to develop things together.

One of the most interesting things I read about the death of Diana was why was there such mourning for her, particularly by women. I think it was Germaine Greer who said that in fact women were mourning for themselves, because she represented themselves to them, it was so similar to their own lives. They had married someone who they felt didn't love them and they spent a lot of time and pain conforming to a model that society had imposed upon them. But I still think that because women now have more choices, their lives are happier than they were. At least I'd like to think so.

I have only two or three close friends that I see about once a fortnight. I would share most of my aspirations with them. Not all, but most. The women that I'm close to have similar lives to me and similar aspirations. Having my life exposed in *Tall Poppies* was quite dramatic. I wanted to go and hide. Even now it's not the sort of thing that company directors do. Looking back now though, I'm very glad I did it.

mother's day

Eve Mahlab was not just an only child (like me), she also had a difficult relationship with her mother. She knew that she was not the daughter her mother wanted her to be but she steadfastly refused to be anyone other than herself. Mother–daughter realtionships are often difficult, particularly if the daughter refuses to lead her mother's life or the life her mother would like her to lead.

Mothers often say that they want their daughters to have all the chances they missed out on; they want us to have more choices. But when we choose a life different to theirs, a life that they perhaps feel cheated of, they see it as a rejection, not just of their life, but of them. They can be resentful, or even jealous.

There is often a lot of repressed anger between mothers and daughters. Sometimes it seems as if mothers want us to lead the same lives they have had, in order that we are similarly punished. There is often a great fear among daughters that we may become our mothers and we resist any tendency in this direction. On the other hand we never stop secretly trying to please our mothers. The mother in our heads still makes us feel guilty.

Eve felt that her difficult relationship with her mother affected her ability to mother her own children.

Only daughters certainly have more pressure on them than those with siblings. At times I think my mother could hardly believe I was really her daugher—we were so different. Even when I made a special effort to please her somthing usually went wrong. Especially on that day of the year she loved, the day she considered her special day to be feted as a mother. I learned that laughter not anger was a better way of coming to terms with it.

Grand occasions were never a strength in my family.

An only child of middle-aged parents who seemed to have nothing in common but me, I knew almost from the beginning that I was responsible for their well-being. And their happiness.

I knew when I was four and made to lie down in the afternoons. I knew by the slant of the sun through the faded blind and the sluggish silence. I knew why my mother had ended up here in the sleeping suburbs. And I swore it would never happen to me.

Lucky, the children of mothers who don't believe in Mother's Days. Easy, when little, to get through. Breakfast on a tray, white flowers, and a card with a big red heart. Perhaps a few trinkets chosen from Woolworths, paid for with saved and precious pocket money. Later on it wasn't so easy. No grandchildren. Just the three of us.

I took them out. To restaurants of my choice, where the day was never mentioned. Daunted by the silver service and which knife and fork to use, they smiled a lot but didn't say much.

To restaurants of their choice we went, with five courses, a white flower for all the mothers in the room, and a person at an electric organ playing requests.

But one day such rituals were no longer possible. Now that walking had become a difficulty and eating seemed to have become the vehicle through which my mother chose to voice her protest against the world. When she could take up to half an hour to eat her morning egg, restaurants were out.

But out was where my mother wanted to go. Not that I could blame her. Domiciliary care and Meals on Wheels were the high spots in her day. Her husband preferred his chooks.

Knowing the day was looming, I asked my mother where she would like to go this year.

'A drive, a nice drive in the country. It's good to get out and see the world.'

I asked my mother what she would like to eat.

'A Big Mac.'

Was she sure?

'I want one with everything, just like on the telly.'

Knowing the Honda Civic wasn't big enough, I rang a hire-car company. The governor had booked their only Mercedes. I settled for next best, a Chrysler LTD.

The day dawned sunny.

The day did not dawn.

The day settled around me like a noose. I could feel the rough male kiss of rope on my neck. I thought of taking a Valium, but remembered the Christmas when it rendered me speechless and unable even to get the turkey out of the oven. Drink was out, as I had to drive. Food was out, as I was on a diet.

'You're late,' said my father.

'Half an hour late,' said my mother.

'I had to pick up the car,' I said.

'Could have used mine,' said my father.

'Whose car is it?' said my mother.

'I hired it.'

'Waste of money,' said my father.

I had to back the car out of the driveway. Mother's walking frame would not fit between the fence and the car door. Patiently I steered Mother towards the back seat. Mother was wearing her new pantsuit. Trousers were now essential, to cover up the swollen arthritic knees. As we edged our way, snail-like, along the cement path I noticed that her make-up was slightly out of alignment. Her eyebrows had that permanently surprised look. My heart leapt into my mouth. This day was Mother's Big Day. They had tried to give me their best, and now it was my turn.

'You look very smart today, my darling.'

'If you say so, my dear.'

One step too many and Mother had managed to wedge herself, or rather her frame, in the gutter. She started to fall backwards.

'Lean forward, Mum.'

'What, dear?'

Catching her with both hands. 'For Christ's sake, Mum, lean forward.'

'Don't speak to me like that, dear.'

I thought my back might break with the weight.

'She ain't heavy, she's my mother.'

'What's that, dear?'

Fearing total collapse.

'Fucking lean forward.'

'I won't have you using that language'—listed at what now seemed a 75 degree angle.

Safely inside the car, Mother continued. 'All the education we have given you and you still talk like someone from the gutter.'

'That's where you would have been, Mother, if I hadn't been so strong.'

'I would rather have fallen than heard those words come out of your mouth. And on Mother's Day.'

We crawled through the Sunday afternoon traffic with Father barking out driving instructions.

'Your presents are in the back window, Mother.'

Father seized them. A territorial imperative.

'They're mine,' Mother said.

'I'll help you,' he said, ripping the paper off the largest one. 'Another pantsuit,' he said, dropping it in her lap.

'You've torn the paper.'

'What do you want to keep that for? Bloody stuff all over the house.'

With grim determination her crooked hands smoothed out the wrapping paper and folded it neatly.

'When are we going to eat?'

'Soon, Dad, soon.'

Desperately scanning the graveyard of used-car lots for a giant 'M', I wondered if it really was possible to kill yourself by jumping out of a moving car. With my luck I'd end up in a wheelchair, a living testimony to martyrdom. Every Mother's Day they would bring me white flowers and take me out for a drive. There are some things worse than death.

Saved by a miraculous 'M' looming up at me, I cut across three lanes of traffic and screeched to a skidding stop.

'Jesus Christ,' said Father.

Mother was still attempting to unwrap the other present.

I ran towards the restaurant, carbon monoxide ballooning my nostrils.

'What's this, dear?' said Mother, eyeing off the bag I handed her.

'It's what you asked for—Big Mac, french fries and an apple pie. Eat it while it's hot. Same for you, Dad.'

'I didn't ask for this, dear.'

'Yes, you did, Mum.'

'When did I?'

'Eat it while it's hot,' said Father, tucking his hankie into the top of his collar.

We sped down South Road. Turning up the radio to drown out the rhythmic clack of loose dentures, I wondered if perhaps I was premenstrual. Is it possible to create a world record for the length of time it takes to eat a Big Mac? Mother clearly had no notion of the term fast food. An hour later I reminded myself to contact the *Guinness Book of Records*.

'This looks like a nice spot for afternoon tea,' I said, as I could wait no longer for a glass, or several, of the champagne that I knew was in the hamper. Better to risk the breathalyser than face a murder charge. Water torture had nothing on the gnawing of a Big Mac.

Unable to lay my hand immediately on the champagne corker, I pulled the cork out with my teeth.

'Champagne, Dad? French. Bought it specially.'

'I'm a beer man myself. It's wasted on me, that good stuff.'

The champagne was cold. So, too, was the water in the thermos.

'What a shame. I was so looking forward to a cup of tea,' said Mother.

'You haven't finished your lunch yet,' said Father.

Like a Japanese train we shot through the countryside, my parents hardly daring to look right or left. Fields and forests flashed by. I concentrated on the white line dividing the grey bitumen.

Side by side in the velvet luxury of the back seat, they slept. I saw them in the rear-vision mirror. Wrinkled faces flushed with the warmth of the car heater. How many times as a child had I nestled into the softness of my mother, or felt the strong arms of my father lift me gently out of the car. Even in my youngest days, they always took me with them to parties.

I saw in the mirror a mother who had loved to dance. A mother who had loved to bake. A mother who had loved to sew. A mother who had loved.

When they bought their first car, a Morris Minor, I had insisted on sitting between them. A cushion specially placed by my father on top of the handbrake. The three of us together . . . in the front seat.

Facing the road ahead.

ROBYN ARCHER
Singer, actor, writer, musician, director

Only child from an Adelaide working-class family. Very ill with chronic asthma as a child. Her comedian/singer father encouraged her to sing and she started performing with him at charity shows. Parents were so pleased she survived her illness that she always felt treasured and special. Always pushed herself to come top at school. Graduated in Honours English then became a nightclub singer, a high school teacher, a national and international singer, writer and performer.

Believes totally in herself and always trusts her instincts. Has no role models but is always confident of what she is doing and where she is going. Comfortable with her sexuality, having chosen tentatively at 15, finally at 25, to be with women, but loves men as working colleagues. Feels at home anywhere in the world, embraces risk and change, loves travel, photography and new experiences but has maintained very close links with her parents and family.

Rushcutters Bay, Sydney, Harbourside

It's a herculean task to pin Robyn down long enough in one spot to have a decent talk. When she's not travelling the world in search of fabulous artistic events to bring to the Adelaide Festival, she's negotiating other areas of her life, like singing, composing, directing or just trying to get together with her partner in the same city for a few days. It's an exciting and exhausting life but the woman who blew into breakfast and gave me a big hug and a kiss was clearly thriving on it. Mind you, she says she's at her best in the mornings. Don't ever try to talk to her much after nine at night because she'll be tucked up in bed, asleep. And don't even think of asking her to a New Year's Eve party, as she's never made it to midnight yet.

She had just returned from travelling halfway around the world. She listed the countries for me. I was exhausted just listening. The thought of negotiating all those airports is enough to put any sane person into a sweat of anxiety. But not our Rob, as her family calls her. They are always amazed and reassured that no matter where she goes in the world, how many important people she meets, how many successes she has, she is always the same old Robyn. In the backyard of her mum and dad's modest home at a family barbie in Adelaide, they look hard at her for any detectable change of accent or slight affectation, and then they hear her throaty laugh and they say to each other, 'She never changes, our Rob, does she? She never changes.'

And there is a sense in which they are right. Of course she changes and develops and expands all the time—she is always open to new ideas and new experiences. But the essential core of that only child, the little girl with life-threatening asthma who took it all in her stride and was determined to be as special as her parents thought she was, is still in evidence.

The little girl who was thrown out of the school choir for singing out of tune simply believed in her father's teaching and started performing with him at RSL club charity shows. At weddings he sang 'Ave Maria' for the Catholics and 'Because' for the Protestants. She firmly believes everyone can sing, because it's all about learning and willpower. Whatever Robyn decides to do, wills herself to do, she will do succesfully. And if she doesn't

get there the first time, she will try again. This is the mark of all successful
people: knock them down and they simply get up and try again.

Breakfast over, she was off to work on the Gay Games and then back
to Adelaide for a few days, then Melbourne, then Hobart, then London,
New York and Paris, then back to Sydney. I went home to bed.

I always get things the second time. I went into the last year of high
school and then the head prefect left school to go into a job and I
became the head prefect. I got the Adelaide Festival not the first time,
but second time. I got the Keating Fellowship, not the first time, but
the second time. Not getting things helps you bounce back. It always
feels like it's the end of the world, but I'm not very good at holding
grudges either. I've got too much to do positively to spend a lot of
energy being grudgy. Takes an awful lot of effort to hate and I really
can't. There are a couple of instances in my life where people really
did me bad. They are rare but one of them I met recently and I
couldn't pretend that I hated them. The ability to do a lot in your life
depends very much on what you do with your talent and your energy.
If you spend a lot of it trying to sow seeds of disaster or hanging
around hating, you can't do it. It just takes too much time, I'd rather
put that all to positive use.

I'm a big finisher. I don't like to leave anything hanging. I like to
get it done and then put it away. Being a singer, I went back to get a
teaching degree because I knew then that you needed that for a
backstop. I'm never short of ideas, which is my best currency, and
that's not changing. When you hit middle age, you think, Is it all
going to go away? But as the body starts to break down in subtle ways,
it's really quite refreshing that you can keep your workload going and
that the ideas are actually stronger, with more depth to them, than
twenty years ago. I overcommit my brain. Sometimes you make a
mistake. I'm a little bit bad about not allowing a 20 per cent factor
for other people's slackness because I tend to programme the way I

would get things done. Of course that's not always the way other people work and if something falls down from some other area then that can really implode.

I'm trying to assemble some teams to do the extra couple of things that I'm going to be doing in the next few years so that I can delegate much more. There's a terrific team to implement the cultural program we've plotted for the Gay Games in October/November 2002—the games themselves take about five days and the cultural events will take about ten days—and there's the new festival for Tasmania, Ten Days on the Island. It's very much a pilot to see whether Tasmania can actually sustain some sort of cultural celebration. I'm sure it can. I have a number of singing gigs (including New York) and now there's the Melbourne Festival in 2002 and 2003.

I have the same agent but they do everything for me. I don't live anywhere. They either forward it to me or they pay it and I pay them afterwards. They're marvellous.

I had a big house in Sydney and I eventually persuaded the co-owner, Di Manson, to buy me out because she was a bit more fond of it than I was, and I didn't want to live there any more. She's living and working successfully in New York now. I bought another, smaller terrace in Lilyfield straightaway. I've got a flat in Bondi but I've not lived in either of them. Everything is in storage and when I'm in Sydney I stay with my partner of almost eight years, Erika Addis. She's a cinematographer, originally from Adelaide. That works, with difficulty. We've tended to have to meet in really odd places, like I was coming back from one of the festival trips, she was shooting in Vietnam, so I called through Vietnam. And we met in Paris last year and this year. Part of the success of the relationship has been because she's always been peripatetic with her work and always got the blame in relationships for not being home. So have I. It's a great combination because neither of us can blame each other for not being around. We equally stuff up our schedules. We'll make plans and then something will change at the last minute and it's been very tricky.

One of the reasons for going back to Adelaide was my parents.

They're marvellous. I recall the theatre company Vital Statistic had a fundraising Doris Day dance down at the Waterside Workers Federation. Dad's 85 and slowing down. He wanted to stay home and watch the football but I took Mum. She's unreal, she still plays four or five sets of tennis on Tuesday. She's 77. She goes line-dancing Saturday afternoon with the girls. Mum and I danced all night together but she was still going at nearly midnight. She's going like a bomb. I'm on permanent stuff for my asthma but it's very good treatment. It's fairly sophisticated these days so I'm not on these Ventolin puffers all day. I don't really worry about it. I don't get any sicker than anyone else. In fact I think I'm healthier than most people. I tend to avoid colds. Maybe once every two years I have an attack. Cigarette smoke is usually to blame.

I walk as much as I possibly can. I'm better when I'm singing because then I really have to shape up and do vocal exercises and then I breathe a lot better. Part of my body is about having a big sing every now and then and the energies flow a lot better when I do that. I've got a reduced lung function but I do a lot with that. I did an article for the Asthma Association where I said I always feel like the asthma has been something to stop me being a monster, because if I didn't have it, I'd need to be caged up. It's a sort of a limiter. I look at a friend who's an epileptic, and I see her being super sensitive, just physically. She can hear conversations ten tables away and isolate sounds in recordings. She really is super-human, but of course every now and then that fuses and overloads. Sometimes I think that my disease is a bit better because it's just put a few limiters on me so that I don't blow out dangerously. So I'm quite grateful about my disease and I'm perfectly happy with it.

I guess the only thing that would push me over the edge would be a series of professional setbacks. For a week or a day or a year, of course you can be off and be unhappy, but nothing has ever sent me into an oblivion of drug-taking or endless bingeing or something that's been unresolvable. Even when I go through a patch of professional disappointment, if I suddenly get a run of shows that don't go so well,

I'm very quick to say, 'Well all right, they didn't like it, so all right, I still like what I did. If they didn't like it, I'll just get on with it.'

I've just been trying to think what I value most and I've been pinning it down lately to the idea of curiosity. I would hate it if I ever stopped being curious about things because I think in the end that's what drives you. It's about the joy of travelling, it's about the joy of picking up a book and sticking with it, it's about being in the thick of a whole lot of ideas and that sense of being curious about what happens in the world. I would really throw it all in if I suddenly looked at myself at some point and thought, You've lost your curiosity, you just don't want to know any more. You see a lot of people like that, who really have tired of ideas.

I have great faith in the brightness of the world. I see kids coming up who are going to find all kinds of solutions. It's just crazy for people my age, or even younger, to be whingeing about the state of the arts, because another generation will find its own answers. There will always be art and sometimes that's a rather dangerous thing to say because there is a bit of a feeling that unless enormous government subsidy goes into it, there won't be any art. But that's complete nonsense. It's preferable for governments to invest in the arts. It means that enormous steps can go forward, particularly in places where our culture was uprooted or clashed with an indigenous culture. It's good that subsidised companies exist and it's great that there are training grounds for people, but if that doesn't exist, something else will. I go to the theatre an enormous amount for work but if I have a day off I am much more inclined to go to an art exhibition, have dinner, go to a bookshop. I think a lot of young people are experiencing their arts in that way.

Catherine Carter, a young director who works at the Centre for Performing Arts in Adelaide, had a bright idea that she would apply for an emerging artists grant, just to dog my footsteps and see what it was like to programme a festival. My response was, well, that's all right, but you understand that you get the money to come on the trip with me and I'm not going to make any arrangements. My secretary will tell you when the meetings are. If you turn up, then I'll introduce you to the people, but I am never going to worry about whether you're there or not and I'm not going to take care of you and I'm not going to baby you, but if you want to do it, by all means. I got a huge shock that she actually got the grant. Of course, as I got to know her more I got less mean and started to enjoy spending time with her and having her around. She'd shoot questions on the local and the national scene.

Suddenly she says, 'Oh, there's been a bit of a change of plan, I'm pregnant.' What followed has been really interesting. She said, 'I'm in a really strong relationship and I want to do this.' So she didn't do her big international trip of a lifetime. They got married, went to Kangaroo Island for their honeymoon and bought a house all in the one day. Her husband, an arts worker, got a steady job. When I went round there the other night he cooked. They both looked after the baby—they had a system whereby if she was going out of her mind, she would ring him at work and say, 'Come and get the baby now.' She's now the artistic director of Come Out, the youth festival.

When I look at somebody like that I think actually the system is not too bad. I also look at a lot of younger lesbian women at the moment and think how much easier it is. I would have had a baby, I'm sure. Early. The systems are such that now you can do anything. My goddaughter, Kes, the daughter of blues singer Lee Sappho in Perth, is just fantastic because she got a job when she was sixteen and she had a boyfriend when she was sixteen. Some nights they'll sit around and watch television and Kes says, 'Oh, I want to go out to dinner with so and so', and he'll say, 'Oh, I don't want to do that,' and she says, 'Righto, suit yourself', and goes out with the girls. I see evidence everywhere where many things have changed.

At the same time I have to say that I think in the positions of real power there is still rank sexism going on. I see evidence of the famous dick-linking that goes on, and that boys still somehow always manage to go with the boys. I'm convinced that they just work in a really different way. By and large the only boys I've worked with are nice ones. I'm now more and more convinced about the differences between women and men in their work patterns. There is this proven mass of connectors between one side of the brain, or one set of brain functions and another, that women have and men don't. We just have literally thousands more connectors. That seems to make sense in lay terms about women constantly seeing the implications of what they do, whereas men with only a few simple connectors say, I'll do it, hang the consequences. I think that's the stuff about war. Thatcher came and disproved all that. But it was her denying that side of her woman-ness that really made her like a man.

Many women in business actually cut off what they consider the weaker aspects. Working in cultural sectors, almost every time I hear a man say this person is too hands-on, he's always talking about a woman. Because women actually want to take care of detail. Like men don't see the dirt. Women have a massive capacity for looking at detail that men actually can't be bothered with. Men have learned that they have to protect that way of working, that it all has to be very straight and you can't have time to dither around. Globally, the directors of all the best festivals are women. Without question. But where's the real power? It's still with the blokes. That's the most heartbreaking aspect of women's position. Carmen Lawrence, Bronwyn Bishop, Ros Kelly, Joan Kirner were just done over by a male machine. It begs the whole question about who would want to be in politics anyway. Probably the best work has been done outside the political circle.

I had no financial education of any kind. I'm an absolutely typical baby boomer. My parents don't own property and have been frugal, have never had a credit card. About the time when I got the creative fellowship those issues were being drawn to my attention. I started to see a lot of my peers on a very direct line to poverty, frankly. I'm better now with money. At least I'm in a better position than I was nine years ago. I support Mum and Dad. I've been buying the car for them. I take them on holidays, out to dinner, buy their theatre subscription. I give them a quality of life that they wouldn't have if they were just impoverished pensioners. If it was only me I could probably just sit, do nothing and be very frugal. I'd probably stay at Henley Beach for a year and I'd be very happy doing that if I really needed to suddenly stop.

It was quite difficult for many of us as artists, looking at other people who had simply gone into fairly dreary jobs, with houses paid off, people who were retiring at 50, 45, just saying, I've had enough, I've got enough money to do it. You turned around and thought, but I've been working sixteen hours a day for twenty years. Our inability to plan for the future is about our great incapacity to imagine ourselves old. At every point in our careers, baby boomers have been the biggest population. As we get older I trust the most horrific aspects of nursing homes are going to be solved and euthanasia will be legalised. There will simply be too many of us. We'll just say, 'I've had a great time. Let me sit on the beach and I'll have a massage and pop me one and off I go.' Absolutely wonderful.

There's a great confidence in being fortunate enough to be with a strength of numbers in that post-war generation. I'm still a bit wary of investing in the stock market because I just see it as gambling and I come from a gambling family (Dad's side) where it had caused real tragedies. When I first came to Sydney, the place that I got in Petersham was just around the corner from the German Club. Within a week I was spending 40 dollars a night in the poker machines and I just stopped. I knew I had the gambling gene. I just had to go cold turkey. I'm excessive. I think I've always been completely excessive, obsessive. I need to get on to huge high jags and go for it. It's all toned down now and you do learn to control it. When the hormones start calming down, it makes you stronger mentally.

Everybody says boys think with their dicks, well, I was no different. I just chased sexual highs all over the world and my life was dictated by it. It seems ludicrous now. All that same energy is still there but it goes into thinking positively and looking after your affairs and your finances. I'm completely reactive. I never design what I do. I have lots of ideas within the framework of what I do, but if somebody says, 'Do you want to do this?' I tend to say, 'Yeah, I'll have a go at that.' I'm a drifter of my class, my generation. I just drift and fortunately I make some good choices. But I would no longer decry the kind of people who worked away and have now retired and are now doing really fantastic things. It's just they're doing the really exciting adventurous part later. They've got there. Fortunately, I woke up just in time not to be poverty stricken.

I've been in love, really in love and truly blessed by a quality of love that I can't believe. I have an enduring relationship with most of the people that I've been intimate with. I can't remember a one-night stand with women. Plenty with men until I really fell in love. I need constant stimulation. I'm never bored, ever, but I think the reason that I have had a series of partners is that I just have never really said to myself, 'I'll hang in for this one because it's the right thing to do.' Only once I went to one session with a therapist for one relationship that I was trying to hold on to and she was terrific. She just said, 'In this relationship you're going to have to regard Robyn's career as the third person in this menage.' Sometimes I do make choices as if my work is my wife or my mistress. I have absolute devotion to my work.

I really believe one's capacity for love and letting people in is due to having devoted parents. Knowing that I had these people looking after me all the time and who just loved everything that I did. I was constantly praised. I've got lots of colleagues and friends who are only children and I think we are selfish little brats a lot of the time, with a highly developed sense of ego. You do have an incredibly strong sense of self. When you've got parents that love you, I think you grow up with this immense capacity for doing for others what they did for you, and that makes you an incredibly generous lover. It translates in different ways. If it becomes sexual then it makes you a devoted lover and you go out of your way to provide treats and surprises and be ultra-romantic, however that is defined.

There are only a couple of times when I think of what I might have done in other circumstances. One of them is when I am listening to the American singer Marilyn Horne. I hear the voice and I know that my voice is in exactly the same place. Every now and then when I listen to her and sing along in the shower I realise the physical potential that has always been there to create something so perfect. But who in our family would ever have known about learning to be an opera singer? There are a number of powerful men who always thought that my writing or my directing was never as good as my singing and I should have just been a performer. I know that what I do best is performing. I know that I'm very good at it. But the minute I thought of doing something else I had a responsibility to try those other things. I also get bored just being a performer. You're like an athlete. You've just got to concentrate on your body and you've actually got to set your brain aside, even to the extent where you'll be powering along with a bit of writing in the afternoon and say, it doesn't matter how good this bit of writing is, stop it now, go for half an hour's sleep, then start to do exercises. That's why when somebody says, 'would you like to do this?' I think, 'Oh all right, I'll have a go. I have no idea but I'll have a go.'

Lonely? Almost never. I've been so busy and so exposed most of the time that being able to be by myself, just with no one, is great. My idea of luxury is a day without appointments. Now and then in the last four years I've been a little bit sorry for myself when I've hit a major crisis within the festival and it's been really tough, and you just think, Oh God, when most people go through these kind of crises they've got their partner there to share these problems with. It's the pillowtalk you miss. I don't think I've ever been bored in my life. There's that endless truckload of books waiting that you've bought and haven't read. There's always a thousand things to do.

Would I come back as a man? I think I've already had the best of both worlds. I might come back as a heterosexual woman next time. I've had the privilege of living a life in a society where it's been possible to take a lot of the best of what men are deemed to have and that is a proactive direction of my career, making the choices myself, being in control rather than being controlled. I think everybody's sexuality is up for grabs. But I actually enjoy being a woman liking men. Some, of course, are assholes and some are completely hateful but actually I like there being an opposite sex to enjoy. I particularly enjoy their differences because I'm not enslaved to them. Being a lesbian and making that choice terribly early has allowed me to enjoy men. Sometimes you meet heterosexual women friends who just slag off men all the time and you keep saying, well, why bother?

John Gaden, the actor, told me that once you get to 40 everybody under 25 is beautiful, and that's true. When you're sixteen, you're so picky and there's only one boy in the class you like, and now I would look at the whole school and think, You're all beautiful. Being very clear about my choices and what I wanted for myself has actually enabled me to be a genuine appreciator of the opposite sex. I love having breasts. I love all the stuff about being a woman. The idea of actually having a doodle in the front that you have to take care of all the time is not of interest. I'd rather not.

I'm amazed that I never got pregnant. I was completely careless, so I could have gotten pregnant any time between about thirteen and 26. Occasionally you do think it was a mistake not to have kids. When I look at my mum and dad and I think, As sweet as they are, there's actually nobody other than me that can look after them with that kind of unconditional love. I'm the only one that can look past their wrinkles and their foibles and the things that I love and hate and still be there, without question.

I was on a flight from New York back to Europe, sitting next to this wonderful New York woman. She said, 'Have you got children?' And I said no. 'Oh, you've got to have children because they'll look after you in your old age.' I thought, She's actually quite sensible. People ask, 'Weren't you lonely and didn't you miss brothers and sisters?' I say no. In fact for me it's fantastic, because if I'd had them, I wouldn't have got the education I did. There wouldn't have been enough money.

Sometimes I do think I never need to meet another person. I don't have enough time for the ones that I like already. This weekend I reckon I met 25 people I've never met before, in Hobart. I'm probably going to meet a hundred today and next week in Tasmania I'll meet another hundred. Privately I'm actually a bit of a bastard. Erika knows, even with those of our friends that I really love, I usually say I can't commit. I say, plan it and if I feel that I can come, I'll come. But actually if you're spending fourteen hours just focusing on new people and ideas, the last thing you can cope with is then going to what's meant to be your relaxing time with another set of ideas. You feel like you're performing all the time. I don't want to sit there like a dag. In that sense I can retain a bit of the diva by saying I want to be alone. But you can't avoid being attracted to ideas. I am fortunate to keep having this amazing parade of humanity before me of all kinds of backgrounds and ages. I have to be open to that. But it's hard work too.

I'm basically just happy to have made it alive this long. You can't not be conscious that your body's getting harder to handle. Occasionally I am driving and I see the full light on my skin and it's crinkling. But what fascinates me, and what I hadn't really expected, was that as I see that happening, so the mind is strengthening. If you can just feel that process of aging and take note of it, it can be every bit as fascinating as the process of growing was. It's almost like an onset of wisdom. Maybe this is what wisdom means. It's not having the knowledge of every book in your head, it actually means an innate sense of better timing, of conserving energy. For all I know that's what 500 years ago people were talking about.

In terms of physical energy, when I get an opportunity I just sleep like a log. I can sleep for twelve hours and I just love it. I almost never use an alarm any more because I wake up two minutes before the alarm is to go off. On the other hand, if I only have five hours sleep I can still get through the day and fire all day and these things are wonderful surprises. This is the miracle of watching the way you change as you age.

wedding day

At the time both Robyn Archer and I were growing up in Adelaide, girls were expected to marry. Morover, they were expected to make a suitable match, to choose someone their parents would feel comfortable including in the family. Weddings were huge productions, often organised around the expectation of the mothers. Over a third of these marriages never lasted. The ritual of the wedding day, however, has. A huge industry is based on the fantasy of true love, forever. Even if the bride has any last-minute doubts, she will inevitably go through with the wedding because of the arrangements and the expectations. An increasing number of younger women are choosing not only not to marry but to live alone. This is a big departure from the traditional history of women in our society.

Robyn Archer chose not to marry, not just because of her sexuality but because of the kind of life she wanted to lead. As a singer, writer, musician and director, the life of the traditional wife and mother would not have worked for her. She wanted to be free to create and invent her life as opportunities presented themselves. She continues to travel, to explore new aspects of her talents, to be the centre of her life. By not marrying she has never been 'the other', she has always been 'the one'. She has been free to follow her work wherever it has taken her. In a sense she has led a man's life, in that her female partners have had to accept that her career comes first.

Her rocks of support, in terms of unconditional love, are her parents. An only child raised in working-class Adelaide (as I was), she always felt an equal part of a unit of three. Her friends were automatically her parents' friends too.

If Robyn had chosen to marry, I suspect her wedding could have been very similar to this one.

No one today would understand why my mother and father thought it such a tragedy that I, their one and only child, should be marrying Timothy. In all other respects he would have been considered a suitable match. Except that he was a Roman Catholic. They insisted on including the word 'Roman' whenever they spoke of it because it conjured up the foreign: the popery, the incense, the candles, the statues with bleeding hearts and trickling blood.

Not that they were religious in the sense of church going. But church to Jean and Jack meant the Church of Christ. A spare hall, no altar, long pews with no carved adornment and nothing on the walls except a clock and an honour roll of those fallen in the wars. At the far end, almost hidden from view, was the baptismal bath into which pubescent girls and boys were fully immersed once they had declared Jesus Christ as their Saviour. Both Jean and Jack had been dunked when they were twelve years old, but much to the dismay of Aunt Maureen, who, unlike the others, had never left the church even though she had left the state, I had never succumbed. Not that I hadn't tried my best to feel the spirit of the Lord come into my heart and fill me with absolute faith. I had tried. I had stood steadfastly and earnestly in those plain pews among those plain folk and promised myself that if 'the call' came, I would follow it. But to the deep disappointment of my Sunday school teachers and, the church elders, and the despair of Aunt Maureen, I had never felt the urge to leave my seat on a Sunday night. It was always at the evening service that the minister, dressed in a badly cut, double-breasted navy suit, pleaded with his congregation. He even implored when persuasion was not enough. Every Sunday night someone in a highly excitable state would succumb and walk down that long aisle to the minister, who would beam like an encyclopaedia salesman who has just clinched a deal. Grasping both hands in his, in case she changed her mind and fled, he'd say, 'Praise be to the Lord, that he has chosen this night to come into your heart, sister.'

I didn't have any sisters or brothers and was convinced that if I had to choose someone as surrogate kin, it would certainly not be anyone in the local congregation. Never had I seen such dour people who so consistently talked of the joy that having Jesus in your heart gave you. The women wore no make-up, had faces like blunt axes and haircuts to match. Among my age group I was the only one who hadn't been baptised on a Sunday morning, dressed in a plain white surgical robe and bathing cap. I was the only one who hadn't emerged from that cold white porcelain, gasping for air, to the sounds of the congregation singing 'Up From The Grave He Arose'. And my peers were not pleased. I felt their eyes like sharp instruments pricking and prodding me to leave my seat. I stood firm. So firm that one Sunday night the double-breasted navy suit appeared before me and said, 'We are very disappointed in you.' And I knew then that I would never return.

Ten years later, when Timothy and I had to decide whether we would have a formal wedding, and if so, where would we hold it, the Church of Christ was never a consideration. Nor was the local Catholic church, Timothy having declared himself an atheist to Jean and Jack, who weren't quite sure whether this wasn't in fact worse than being an RC. Both families pleaded with us to at least have a 'proper' wedding, even if it wasn't to be in a church. And so it was that in December 1968, in Adelaide, in Jean and Jack's back garden, we were to be married by a celebrant. Like most compromises, it pleased no one.

Jack had roped off the chooks that normally roamed among the vegetable garden, and he'd attempted to camouflage the garden with metres of striped canvas, ropes and tent pegs. He'd had to improvise like this in the desert during the war, he told Jean, who had expressed her concern that he hadn't rung the 'proper' tent people. It wasn't that he was mean; he just didn't see any point in wasting money on unnecessary frills. And after all, he had already paid for a large marquee that he and a few mates had erected while consuming many bottles of beer. (Erection, he'd learned, was extra.) The one thing he didn't mind paying for was the keg. I did have a battle with him over the champagne, which he insisted was all just sweet bubbly anyway. He had taken the initiative and ordered a hundred bottles of pink Barossa Pearl. 'Match the bridesmaids' dresses too,' he'd added, obviously thinking this logic would clinch the argument.

My two bridesmaids, Penny and Jenny, had in fact chosen a hot-pink shot taffeta, which I'd argued might be too 'hot' given the month, but they insisted, especially as it would match the pink Sobranies we were all addicted to smoking. Penny said it would also come in handy at the next bad-taste ball; after all she was a communist, didn't approve of bourgeois celebrations and was a veteran of three anti-Vietnam demonstrations. Jenny was Timothy's younger sister. She was still at high school and believed anything Penny said.

My mother had spent the last month with a mouth full of pins. A milliner before she married, she had insisted on making my veil, and the pins prevented her from telling me what she really thought about my marriage. But the eyes said what the pinched lips repressed. As Timothy was the eldest of seven, his mother, although disapproving, was relieved to get him out of her overcrowded war-service house, and at least they didn't have to pay for the reception. Apart from discussing guestlists and honeymoon arrangements, Timothy and I had hardly spoken to each other. Both of us were finishing off the teaching year and had marking, school reports and staff farewells at our separate schools.

The day was suddenly upon us. At 6 am my father brought me a cup of tea and the news that it was going to be a 'real stinker, well over the forty degree mark'.

'Oh great,' I mumbled, feeling a rim of sweat gathering at my hair line.

'Just as well I ordered that extra keg. I bet those micks will drink till the cows came home, especially when it's free.'

'Yeah, right, Dad,' I mumbled, already taking the line of least resistance.

'Cheer up, me girl. Supposed to be the happiest day of your life.'

'I know, Dad, just give me a chance to wake up. Where's Mum?'

'Still in bed. Says she thinks she's got one of her migraines coming on.'

I spent the morning shaving my legs, scraping my armpits, plucking my eyebrows and trimming my pubes. No stray hair was safe, except for the tresses that would eventually have to be teased within an inch of their lives in order to form the beehive. Penny and Jenny arrived at noon bearing bags of cold champagne and hairspray. As we sipped and teased and sprayed each other's hair, bayoneting the wayward clumps with French pins, I entertained a sneaking suspicion that this might be fun after all.

'Tim's got the most humungous hangover,' volunteered Jenny. 'He was chundering all morning and Mum said she'd have to call the doctor if he didn't stop.'

'Really.'

'Dad said it was just as well the wedding was outside, so he could run behind the daisy bush,' she chuckled.

By the time the three of us had finished with our busbies we could have done the Changing of the Guards at Buckingham Palace. My mother had finally risen from her bed and was encased in a mauve silk dress with a matching hat that almost covered the expression on her face.

'Come on, Jean, you're not going to a hanging,' said Jack, looking very jolly in a new suit.

'Do your top button up and straighten your tie,' was my mother's response.

'Jeez, it's a scorcher! Give a bloke a break.'

'Jack, this is your only daughter's wedding,' continued my mother, her voice teetering on the edge of a sob.

'All right, all right, just don't go getting over-emotional. There'll be enough of that when your sisters arrive.'

'Don't you start about my sisters.' The colour of her face was beginning to mirror her hat.

'Come on, you two, give it a rest today, please.'

They both disappeared up the passage mumbling to themselves. My bridesmaids helped me into my dress, which had daisies made from guipure lace appliqued over the bodice. Too much champagne and no air-conditioning meant that the entire dress felt as though it was appliqued to my body. Layers of pancake make-up barely hid the fact that our complexions matched the taffeta of the bridesmaids' dresses, not to mention the overflowing ashtray of Sobranie stubs. I was beginning to feel more than a little nauseated.

My father knocked on the door, entered, pronounced us all the most beautiful girls he had ever seen, then asked Penny and Jenny to leave us alone. Closing the door behind them, he hugged me so hard I thought my bones would break. When he finally pulled away I saw tears in his eyes. He took out a clean white handkerchief and blamed the heat.

'Now listen, sweetheart. Everything's ready. The tent looks a picture. They've done us proud with the flowers. There's enough food to feed the Arabs. Everyone's here, all your mother's sisters, even mad Maureen has flown in from Sydney specially. The mick rellies look a bit on the rough side and *he* looks like death warmed up.' He paused and lowered his voice.

'But sweetheart, the Holden's out the front. Here are the keys. You can still make a run for it. Don't worry about everyone else. I'll get the grog going and they won't even care after a few.'

He was serious.

'Thanks, Dad, but I'm determined to see it through. I do love Timothy,' I said, with more conviction than I felt.

'I only want what's best for you,.'

'I know that, Dad. Let's get on with it, shall we.'

As we emerged into the dazzle of the three o'clock sun, the University Jazz Band played a barely recognisable version of 'Here Comes The Bride'. Feeling the wet patch already forming in the crook of Dad's arm where I was gripping him, my lobster bridesmaids and I entered the stifling marquee. Timothy was white, clammy and shaky as he took my hand.

'Just try not to throw up,' I whispered through smiling clenched teeth. He did not respond. The celebrant, whom I had never met—Timothy had assured me he 'did' most of the university students—was throwing his hands around in a dramatic manner and his lips didn't help the effeminate rhythms of his syntax.

'Do you take Timothy to be your lawful wedded huthband?'

Every question was underlined by an exaggerated upward inflection. I could hear Penny sniggering behind me.

'Did you have to get Liberace to marry us?' I hissed. Timothy appeared to be suffering from lockjaw.

My mother's sob punctuated the pronouncement of 'huthband and wife'.

With that our sibilant celebrant grabbed me and brushed his lips on both sides of my face and then repeated the process with Timothy, this time lingering noticeably longer. The band struck up and I heard my father say, 'Anyone for a beer?'

Perhaps it was the heat but no one felt like eating the salmon vol-au-vents, asparagus rolls, potato salad and cold collations that had been laid out on trestles at the back of the marquee. The noise level seemed to rise rapidly. Timothy and I did the rounds of the rellies, introducing each other to a series of wet hands and dry lips. I noticed my father doing a roaring trade at the keg and my mother fanning herself with a lace hankie and staring into the middle distance.

A voice at my elbow said, 'Well, married but never baptised.' Aunt Maureen, looking more upholstered than usual in a matching floral ensemble, was not smiling. 'Will the kiddies be brought up Catholic or communist?'

Before I could answer, a microphone crackled to life. My Aunt Sybil called everyone to attention. 'Timothy's family may not know, but our family has a family song and my sisters and I would like to sing it. Come on, girls, join in with me. Out the front here.'

And there they were, even my mother. Trained in the choruses of the Church of Christ, they made up in volume and trills what they lacked in harmony. They were followed by a red-faced bloke in a fawn polyester suit.

'Tim's family also has a family song. Do you know "When Irish Eyes Are Smiling"?' he asked the band.

It wasn't long before Uncle Bill had pushed his way to the front, grabbed the microphone and begun singing 'Three Old Ladies Locked In The Lavatory'. Somewhere in the middle of 'Elizabeth Carter, The Most Phenomenal Farter', my mother swooned against one of the tent poles in either a real or imagined faint. Unfortunately the skills Father had learned at Tobruk had failed him. Mother collapsed onto the lawn, taking the marquee with her as she went. The elaborate arrangement of striped canvas attached to the fence to keep the chooks at bay followed suit. The noise and chaos that erupted as the terrified hens squawked and flapped among the guests and those attempting to reposition the marquee was nothing compared to the siren of the approaching ambulance. Aunt Maureen, who had gone inside to spend a penny, had seen it all through the kitchen window and immediately dialled 999. She always thrived on a crisis.

At ten minutes to seven that evening we were standing on the platform of the Adelaide Station, hugging goodbye to those of our friends and relatives who could still stand up and hadn't been admitted to casualty.

'Just as well the keg was in the shed,' said my father, trying to put on a brave face. My mother was wearing dark glasses and a cloth bandage where once the mauve hat had so smartly sat. Timothy and I were catching the *Overland* to Melbourne, where we would board the *Fairstar* to London and return who knew when. The world was before us.

As I threw my wedding bouquet into the sea of waving hands, my mother's mouth opened, suddenly pin free. Her voice soared above the bouquet and the din: 'I'll be dead before you get back.'

FABIAN DATTNER
Motivational speaker and consultant

Nurtured in a political, artistic, passionate family and community. Youngest and only daughter, with two brothers. Worshipped her father, who told her being female was irrelevant, that she could be anything she wanted. He believed that the orator has the most power in the world. She understood early the power of language, graduated with honours in sociology and started work in a small publishing company. Married, had two children and took them to work with her. A great believer in the maxim that if a system doesn't work, then create a new system, she set up the Second Chance Prisoner Business Register.

She took over the running of her father's fur and leather business, met her second husband and split up with the first amicably. After her father died, she expanded the business, only to become a casualty of the pilot's strike and rising interest rates. The business was sold, together with her mother's house, to pay the debts. She became a keynote speaker and a consultant on change and how to turn adversity into opportunity.

She believes you always have a choice in life. Believes there is a creative solution to every problem. Always involves the staff in business decisions. A great believer in positive feedback.

She has a vision of long-term change in Australia and wants to help ordinary people understand their own capacity for change. Believes that you have to look for what is working, not what isn't; think creatively, overcome fear and believe in yourself.

Her house, Eltham, Melbourne

The usual cold grey wintry skies that greet you in Melbourne. It was a roaring log fire that greeted me in Eltham, in the house that her mother had been forced to sell when Fabian was having trouble with the banks in the 1980s.

Not only had Fabian totally resurrected her finances and used her skills to establish a whole new business enterprise, but she has managed to buy back the family home. Her mother now lives in a small cottage next to the main house, which is big enough for Fabian to have her office and her staff next to the room where we sit. I am very impressed with what she has managed to achieve in the time since we last spoke.

Although she had the flu, or the vestiges of it, she was her usual warm, embracing self, able to establish an instant intimacy and rapport, even though we hadn't seen each other for twelve years. We snuggled down together on the comfy settee. First coffee, then a delicious lunch and a bottle of red were placed on the coffee table in front of the glowing fire, and the whole time we never stopped eating and drinking and talking. Hours went by until I realised I had a plane to catch, but I knew that if I had suddenly decided to spend the night, it would have been organised. We would have gone on sitting there, drinking the wine, pausing only to throw a few logs on the fire as the rest of the family dropped in for a chat. We all would have been embraced in the circle that Fabian has chosen for herself. That's the kind of woman she is.

This was the way she was reared in this house that always had interesting artists, writers or thinkers visiting, eating and drinking, arguing and laughing. She was a child in the halcyon days of Eltham as an artists' colony.

When my cab swept by the famous house, Montsalvat, I wondered what had happened to all that urge to celebrate the artist, to have a community of like-minded souls. Did the death of hippiedom discredit all that? Why are we all tapping away on our computers, all alone in our rooms in our separate homes? We meet for coffee or lunch but rarely do we live together or work together. Or is it all a romantic dream that ends in tears and is mythologised later, like the Bloomsbury set? Is the reality of community life nothing like the idealised version that future generations read about and ache for?

Fabian seems to remember it as a golden period in her life and has tried to recreate it, in the same house, with her extended family and friends. Not that she very often sits around talking all day. She works very hard and is relentless in pursuing her mission. She sincerely believes she is on this earth to make a difference for the better, and there is an urgency about her that only the ravages of the dreaded flu can diminish. It takes a lot of energy to be as positive as she is and to communicate that energy. She has the ability to take risks, to see beyond the present. This forms the basis of her work.

I have a blissful relationship with Ken, my husband, but I look at all the powerful women I know and I don't see many with good relationships. I think we've probably got a fairly skewed idea of what we need. Women think that because they're powerful and successful, they've got to look for a powerful, successful male. As men through millennia have known, you can only really have one person in the family who takes the public domain. Somebody has to hold the fort. It's like we've devalued house and home so tremendously, there's no holding of the centre. For the greater part of our marriage, even now the kids have grown up, he's very much a support role.

The end of 1989, beginning of 1990, the business closed down. All the creditors were repaid. I started working in a variety of unusual situations. It became known in the media that Dattners had been closed down very successfully and that I had dealt with it in a very open and honest way and I had had a very good relationship with the creditors and with the receivers. All my people got placed into jobs and I then made a choice to go and find out what I'd done wrong as a leader. I really wanted to go and talk to people and find out what it is that they wish leaders would do differently. But because I'm also an entrepreneur, I knew I could make a business out of it. The first thing I ran into was this huge gender divide in the concept of success and failure. For men business failure is a terminal experience. For women, it's an experience to learn from. I would have men who would greet me in the street and it would be as if I had terminal cancer. With grief in their expression, they'd say, 'We really admired you and you gave it your best shot. Too bad.' And I'd come away feeling like my life was over, and I was 36. But I'd meet the women and they'd say, 'I really admired the way you handled it. What are you going to do with yourself now, what did you learn?' So from the women I got this sense of it being a part of life, not an end game. And so, having then worked with a lot of people who had really had to face very frightening moments in their business career, and seeing the difference with the way men and women handle it, I wrote my first book, which was *Nothing Ventured Nothing Gained*.

I see myself as a steward, a custodian warrior, and my job is to try and make our world a better place for young people coming on. I see myself as someone who's interested in changing our community for a more sustainable future. Now I have a business that's all about that. Every waking minute of our business is about that. That's the nature of vision and it is that vision that propels your actions.

I was working on my own and slowly moving to organisations who had heard how I managed Dattners. Go and listen to what your people have to say about how you can turn your business around, or how you can change your community, or how you can change a family. Don't feel you are isolated as a leader and that you have to have the solutions. I learned about the danger of entrepreneurs who are on their own without balance. Entrepreneurs, in my opinion, very rarely make good managing directors in organisations, community or otherwise, because almost by nature they live in the future. And without them we don't create anything. Part of the visionary process is the vision which is in your mind's eye as if it were a complete picture, but entrepreneurs or visionaries very rarely get further than 70 per cent of the way to the present. People who are sequential, orderly, pragmatic thinkers very rarely get more than 70 per cent of the way into the future. They can't function without each other. The visionary creates the sense of purpose in the future that the pragmatic, logical, sequential thinker then must build on. Without each other they create nothing.

Part of life is the magic of finding who complements you in life. My father said, you're not going to sell a portion of the business, over my dead body. He was terribly, terribly wrong. Because what holding on to it all does is create sameness, and that means that the business will be brilliant in those areas where you're brilliant and awful in those areas where you are awful. Seventy-five per cent of organisational climate is generated by the leadership and now I have partners who are radically different from me and complement my skills, and I've seen the impact of that on an organisation. We each do well what the other does poorly. It's like diversity in a family, or in a community. We need the courage to be flexible, to look at yourself and say, what could I do differently? Not to blame. We're all good at blaming.

I would have worked personally with over 1400 teenagers in the last ten or twelve months. If only you could be a fly on the wall to watch this experience. It's called Circle of Judgement and it happens on day two of the programme. They sit in a circle and the task is very simple. We've built security so everyone is safe with one another, but your task is simply this: to tell this group what it is like to be judged and found wanting. I can guarantee 45 girls will be in tears about how crippling it is. Judgement is fine if I hold my hand out to you and pull you up and say, 'Good on you, go for it', because then you do. Who's got a goddamn mandate on the right way to do life? The power of your vision adds value to all of us. Your courage adds value to all of us. If we diminish you and make you the same as us, then we diminish all of us. Reinforced almost every day of my life is how we cripple one another with our negative judgement, but if we allow each other the right to experiment and learn through life then we'll build, and instead of intimidating people we'll create capable people.

After the business was wound up my mother lost our family home. We took out a big mortgage on our house, my husband and I moved out into our garage and Mum had our bedroom. Our living room became my office and that's where I slowly started to build my business, and it went on to be very successful. When I look back at it now, I knew then that I had to tell the story of what it was like to have to go through that sort of failure publicly, and that was the motivation behind the first book. I was able to speak at a time when a lot of businesses were freaked out. We're talking early 1990s. I knew what they were going through, so I brought it out into the open.

I'm a very engaging speaker. I don't stand up behind the podium and just read from notes. I started working with organisations from what I believe is the right point, and I wish somebody had done it for me, which is an audit. You go in and you have the courage to listen to what people really think about your organisation. It doesn't matter whether it's a small or community-based organisation, a business or government department—you hear what the people have to say. You dignify their existence by listening. I would interview their people one-on-one. It motivated people within organisations. I rekindled their sense of vision. Also, I now started to share with these people what I'd learned and done well, which was that you've got to anchor the vision to pragmatics.

I interviewed over 5000 people in over 300 organisations in over 30 industries. So by the time I got to 1995–96 I really knew a lot about business. I knew a lot about community. And I knew a huge amount of what people really thought. So I was able to talk to audiences and confidently know that 85 per cent of the people in that audience would feel that for the first time somebody had spoken a truth that they hadn't heard publicly. I would constantly have people come out and say, 'Oh, I'm so glad somebody said this. I thought I was on my own.' It was like the emperor's new clothes. Everyone could see he had no clothing on, but I thought I was the only one who saw that. And I would bring it out into the open and tell people, you're not on your own. Then I would get people to put their hands up to a range of questions I would ask them. And I would say, 'Look at these hands, don't look at me. This is your world, this is your choice, are you listening? What are you going to do differently about it?'

I made an enormous amount of money. There's no shortage of money. You are worth what you think you're worth. I charged what I thought was fair and reasonable and to this day we always guarantee. If you don't like what you get, you don't pay. If you don't feel you got what you paid for, you don't pay. The speaking circuit was no more than maybe 10 per cent of my business. The consulting was by far the big part. Then I felt like I was a dam and I was about to burst. So I wrote my second book, which is *Naked Truth and the Australian Working Community*.

Then I started to get itchy feet and thought, I don't want to be on my own any more. By that stage Mum had bought a house, which we'd been able to help with. We'd got rid of debt and I didn't want to ever go into debt again. So Jim Grant joined me. DGL is now this company, which is Dattner Grant Limited. Then we made a decision to bring in CEOs, managing directors or director—people who really knew what they were talking about, not consultants who'd been through an academic stream. We brought in a young man, Andrew Greatrex, who had been Director of Patient Services at the Repatriation Hospital in South Australia.

I've retained a link with South Australia. I still believe that if you can do it there, you can do it anywhere. I just wish it had another Don Dunstan. Nowhere else in the country have we got the opportunity we've got in South Australia, which is to rekindle the intellectual spirit in this country. It's all money in Queensland, it's fantastic entrepreneurship in Western Australia, pragmatic arrogance in Victoria. Sydney is glitz and glamour. Don Dunstan was a really great leader. And he had that great ingredient, he trusted other people. He took his voice to Australia—he wasn't a parochial leader. In this room we fundraised for him.

This house has seen many wonderful Australians pass through it. How we got it back is a wonderful story. We were having dinner with my mum, who had a house nearby. I said to Ken, I need to see our old family home. I had some strange compulsion to see it. We came around and stood at the gates and it was just heartbreaking. It was clearly needing restumping. The garden, which was one of the most beautiful gardens I've ever seen, was decimated. There was three feet of grass growing, there were lights hanging free. It was so neglected and I was sad because I know we'll never build places like this again. You have to cherish these for posterity. It's about 70 squares. It's huge. We went back to Mum's and told her we'd been to see the property and it was very neglected, and mum said, oh I think that Neil Brown, the ex-Liberal Party politician who owned it, is thinking of selling it.

In my parents' time and the people prior to them, it had always been a spiritual place where people came, and it was shared. So I got a bolt of electricity. A mate of mine in the area was a real estate agent and I said, 'Can you find out if it was on the market?' To cut through all the details, by the following Wednesday we'd bought it. We put both my property and Mum's house on the market, and both sold within two weeks, for considerably more than we would have settled on. It was just fate, we were destined, and we were able to buy it with money to restore it. We came into the house and nothing had changed. After sixteen years of successive owners, I opened a cupboard in the little loo and there was a note there in my mother's handwriting. We went to look downstairs and we got really angry and said, 'Oh God, the bastards haven't cleared out all their junk.' I looked at it and went, 'Oh my God, it's our junk.'

Finally the house started to smile. You could just feel its spirit saying, at last, somebody who will bring life back. That's my mother's studio, her living room. She's a very handsome woman at 82. She'll just read, because she feels like it, all of Shakespeare's plays or Hippocrates. She's amazing. I would protect her and care for her to her last breath. So it's a floating community. My husband and I live here permanently and my sons. My youngest is doing his Year Twelve at school. My big son lives here, in and out. And then there's this floating population of young people and Mum. And the business operates from here as well. We have a lot of programme functions here.

Ken grows 300 bonsai and he's been setting a track record to see how long it takes to get a degree. He's spent seventeen years in and out of university. He's done languages, philosophy. He's now in the third year of psych but I think he's actually decided that he'll stick to it. He keeps the home fires burning. Women may like to be professional but truth be told, we like a cosy fire. We like warmth and sharing a good meal. Our profession isn't everything. Kenny is my best friend, my companion. He's a wonderful man, a strong man, a wonderful lover, and I feel cared for and nurtured. There's always a place in the world where I belong. I sometimes think that men have it lucky because women make wonderful home partners and they nurture, they protect and they preserve in a natural way. That's a challenge for men because that's not the role that they are given. Nor is it easy, I think, for women to let men be men while doing that role.

I lived in this house from five until I left home at eighteen. But this was really where we all came back to. I lost my virginity here. Painters regularly gathered here and my father built an art collection by supporting them. My mother was a painter, too. Portraitist and landscape.

The fourth partner, Joe Forth, who's joined us relatively recently, was the former CEO of Corporate Express. I'll give you an example of the range of environments we can work in. We may work in the custodian programme, which is with the sixteen-year-olds. That's about helping kids to change the world, giving them back a sense of possible future. The schools pay for it or the students do themselves and there are three programmes and then there's a two-year link to our website. The first session is called 'Girls to Women as Leaders'. It's women on their own, so the girls go off with the facilitators who are all senior leaders. We teach them how to teach but we tell these kids the truth about what's happening in the world and we rekindle what vision is about. I plan it, I run it. The South Australian state government has just also taken it on this year and is trialling it. We also do a special programme just for boys. Then we have 'Bridging the Gap', in which we bring the boys and girls together.

I just wish I could wave a magic wand and every leader on the planet would witness what these kids say about their future and the shit these boys have to go through around their role models and how much hate, the win/lose mentality, that football's promoted. They can't say how much they want to touch each other, because you're a poofter in Australia if you touch one another. There are insights into why suicide in boys is so high and what we need to do to redress it and how much we could be role-modelling the leadership of the future with these kids. I know it's sacrilege in Australia, but watch a football final, and what an awful metaphor. He who wins gets all the laudation and he who leaves, leaves crying. What sort of message are we sending our kids? And I see the damage it does to kids.

The third programme, 'Bridging the Gap', is 'what do you want to do differently?'. What do you think? We don't try and push any model onto them. We just create the space where they don't judge each other, and these kids are very astute. They know what needs to be done. The challenge is, what are you going to do differently today as a result of what you've heard? We have a two-and-a-half-year leadership project with the Child Support Agency, which was until recently a big division of the Tax Office. It's now gone over to the Department of Family and Community Services. We've got 80 of their senior leaders from all over the country who meet bi-monthly and we design and run a huge state-of-the-art process around leadership development. But it's not the ten 'you-beaut' ways to be a leader, it's the distinguishing capabilities of exceptional leadership.

High-order reflection simply means time-out to talk. Time to really reflect without feeling frantic, like you have to do something else. It's about the space to not have an agenda but to reflect on our world. If you have no time for reflection, you are constantly 'doing', but who's guiding the future, who's shaping the future? So the challenge is in how to translate high-order reflection into pragmatic reflection. If you don't know what your vulnerabilities are, how can you lead? If you can't know that both your great assets and your great liabilities make and shape the community, how can you lead? It's teaching them to be courageous enough to look at themselves. What is real listening? It's not just sitting in there and nodding your head, it's understanding the spirit of the person opposite you, and that if you diminish one you diminish all of us. It's amazing. It's a transformational process affecting 2500 people. Instead of it just being eight leaders in a rarefied environment, our philosophy is that you have an absolute obligation to take that into your organisation, so an inherent part of it is there are another 400 people who are being taught by the leaders. Each of those 400 people have an obligation to teach the next one, so at the end of the cycle 2500 people are touched by the process.

We do a huge amount of leadership mentoring. We would, between us all, be mentoring, individually, well over 150 leaders. A big part of what we do is create space for leaders to talk about whatever they're afraid of. We've changed our world but we haven't changed how we support leaders. So they're often thrown into the deep end. It's a bit like saying, you're all going to be writers but we're not going to teach you to write. We think one of the things that's happened is that if you isolate the decision-making in our community to a few people, you miss the power of the input of a wide range of people. We don't do that in our communities, and what's happened is that we've got this overwhelming loss of trust.

There's this wonderful new area in psychology called evolutionary psychology and they look at what enables you and I to be the best that we can be. They conclude that the single quality that empowers you and I to be the best, and to do the best that we can, is trust. There've been three watershed pieces of research done in this century around trust. One was done in 1936 in Philadelphia. A whole range of people were asked, do you trust your leaders? Ninety-two per cent of respondents said yes. A similar piece of research was done in 1965 in New York. It was down to about 65 per cent. Good old Griffith University in Australia did one in 1995 and it was down to 35 per cent. What happens in the absence of trust is that we become selfish because we feel we have to look after ourselves.

One of the great things about owning your own business, like writing your own books, is the capacity to constantly change and do exactly what you want, when you want to do it, how you want to do it, with whom you want to do it, on a forever basis. If you asked me what I'll be doing five years from now, I'd have absolutely no idea. I know I'll be fighting for change but I don't know in what domain.

I've worked really, really hard. But I don't think any of my life's been hard. I have a blessed life. I think I'm very lucky. What we do hugely adds value. I don't count the dollars, I don't count my time, I don't say, well, I've given you that much, therefore you owe me that. I'll put in whatever it takes to make the result work, and at every turn there are lots of things that are funded by our business. We have an involvement with a movement in South Africa and we're bringing out a whole lot of kids to Australia next year who have been in prison in South Africa. It's called the Khulisa Project. And I'm still involved with Second Chance, trying to get the scholarships up and running for very young kids who have been in prison. My attitude is that you use what you've got to make happen what you dream of happening and you don't divide it out. Some people have money and they pay you, and some people don't and you use the money you get elsewhere.

Your life is a story but so many people prematurely turn the last page and then sit with a closed book for the rest of their lives where in actual fact we're up to page 375 of a 900 page book. You must keep going. I've met very few women who don't believe they work harder than most men. And I think that's because we actually can. We're lucky because we actually physically can do that and what we will see in the next millennium is a rise of women, because our world needs to be made safe and warm again. It's not a safe, warm or nurturing place, it's a cold, brittle, fragile world where we've managed to make lots and lots of toys but we've also made it a world that is not accessible to, or welcoming to, the majority of people. Now we are laying the groundwork for revolution unless we do something radically different.

There's a rising tide of discontent. Interestingly enough, we think that young kids relate to technology but my experience is that they feel that technology is replacing community and they don't want it to. They're not embracing it. They use it as a tool the way we used a slide rule or a calculator and that's where they want it to stay. They don't want it to rob them of community and they are concerned that technology is taking over. So I think we'll have an emotional revolution in the 21st century, which is people saying, where is the spirit of community? Where is our spirituality? We've created this material world, now what? I think it's natural evolution. I think we're rising to a higher order, we just have to be patient while we get there.

There's not much argument in the scientific community now about the threat that our plants are under. One other thing that I have done in the last nine years is I have poured energy into my own education. Apart from university and courses, I've read and read and read. Hundreds of books. Very impressed with the work of Robert Graves, who held that mankind is evolving despite, but not because of, anything it does, that the evolution of mankind is a series of monumental value shifts. It's always a move *away* from. He said we are only just beginning to taste what it's like to be truly human, to reach the greatness that we're capable of, the recognition that we are capable of compassion as well as creativity as well as invention. We're capable of protecting and preserving as well as inventing and developing, instead of this obsession with gathering and holding and hoarding. When we finally get that message, then we have the capacity to reap heaven on earth. If heaven exists, it will exist on earth.

I've gathered bits and pieces from all over the place. I listen to the anxiety of people like Suzuki fearing that we won't react in time. I'm not optimistic. I'm not pessimistic. I am at various times both. I vacillate. I'm much more emotional and much moodier as I get older. My experience is sufficient to say bastards do win. There is evil in the world and I've met it. But I think human beings will rise to their moment of greatness when faced with adversity. What I'm saddened by is that it will take adversity for us to rise to our own greatness. The adversity we will face is the diminishing biodiversity of the planet. As somebody who spends six weeks a year in real wilderness I've experienced great grief at the prospect that we will lose the biodiversity that we've got, because I think that it's priceless.

What I fear is that the current leadership have got their vision up their bums. I look forward to the shift in leadership which will see a new wave of leaders move in and who care a bit more about a broader range of things other than money. I don't think politics is where change will be effected. I've done too many naughty things in my life to be in politics. I would freak out too many conservative people. I also love my freedom too much.

I don't believe in God. I understand why people need to believe in God. I believe in the spirit between you and me. I believe that there is a deeper truth. I think there's probably an accumulated meaning that is somewhere deep within our genes where we are part of an evolving story. I think Buddhism speaks greater truths to more people than any religion that I've related to. I'm a huge admirer of the Dalai Lama. Not because I think he's reincarnated and is a deity, but because I see a man who embodies compassion and I've felt it in his presence.

I'm on my way to where I want to be. I think I can be very loving and very compassionate, and I really do care about people. But I can become so embroiled in possibility that I don't really listen properly, or I'm already tracking for a solution and you haven't finished saying what you're saying to me and I'm not listening to what you're saying. I'm already thinking of something that could be done differently. And I'm very conscious of that and work hard not to do that. There's a real crying need to be heard. It's compassion that's wanting in our world, not cleverness. We need more time for one another, a little bit more space, a little more grace, a little more awareness of our obligation as a part of, not apart from, a community. I think I'm on my way but I don't imagine I'll really get to where I want to be until I'm a very, very old lady. I saw an old woman who was 96 in a BBC documentary, and she spent time in the hills in Nepal, climbing. The young interviewer says to her, 'Don't you think it's about time to stop?' and this wonderful woman turns to the camera and says, 'For what?'

Without power, very little happens. But there are two different types of power, one of which we eulogise and one of which we don't understand. Personal power, which I have had in abundance and I'm extremely cautious about. If wisdom is needed, it's in the execution of personal power because I know that it is intoxicating and dangerous. Then there's socialised power, which is about your ability to effect change in the society, and for me that's to be celebrated. Organisations like World Vision are based on socialised power. Politics should be based on socialised power but unfortunately it attracts people who are interested in personalised power. I don't think we understand power well in our society but I think it's very, very important. I really celebrate powerful women. I love their company. I really love being a woman.

Sex for me is number one. I'm a sensualist, I love food, I'm very physical. I have a wonderful physical relationship with my husband. Sex is good healthy stuff. I think it's about intimacy. The sexuality that a woman enjoys is a total body experience. I'm a very tactile person and I'm very cuddly with all my family. Intimacy of touch stops us being angry, gets the tension out of our bodies. Three things, they say, we need to prosper into antiquity: a modicum of exercise, intellectual challenge—you have to keep using your brain—and the third is being touched. Physically being touched. Old people, like babies, are dying if they don't get touched. I find sex quite an ugly word. I have a sexuality, I'm very confident with my sexuality, but for me it's intimacy, it's that absolute lock-out time with my partner, where we are just totally focused on one another. Because it's such a strong love, it's an absolute given. I think that's a fine thing to have in your lives. I have a huge need for love. I think that's why people get involved in caring industries. You do something that gives out. How do you feel after you've spoken to an audience who have enjoyed what you said? You're on a high. It's quite addictive.

The choice you make is, do you want to give that love? The capacity to be kind and to be loving can be placed into anyone. You don't have to just have it with your intimate closest, the capacity for clean and pure and unadulterated love resides in all of us.

I have an insanely strong sense of justice. Nothing will distress me more than if that value is trodden on. I've learned that the faster I deal with it, the more effective I can be. Issues of justice eat me up.

My downtime is often spent with young people. I love their absence of judgement. I find a lot of adults really boring. Either they all want to solve my problems or me to solve theirs. I have a very small, select group of adults that I enjoy being with but they're full-tilt players, they're out doing outrageous things and being very entrepreneurial.

I absolutely know I have another 60 years ahead of me and I have no intention of stopping. Live life full-tilt. I love the idea of jousting at windmills and sometimes I take on the real fire. You don't know, until you get there, which will be the illusion and which will be a substance but you do it anyway. Better to have tried and failed than never to have tried at all. Life is to be explored, but I can say with absolute confidence that my partner and I will be together till the day one of us dies. It's that sort of partnership. I also think you accept what love comes your way. It is a blessed thing and I don't think you should argue about who's got the right to give it or who's got the right to receive it. Let's raise our rapiers and put on our patch across one eye and go to the bow of the boat and run the seas. Then I'd be in your company.

I love meeting new people and we have a lot of people here on the weekends. But I'm also one of these people that, right in the middle of the dinner party, if I don't want to be there I'll just quietly get up and leave it. I'm well known for it. My downtime is very precious to me.

I have chosen to join a battle that never really adversely affected me and I've taken it up because I learned that my experience is not a universal experience. I came from a very supportive and privileged background and that is not true for a lot of women. The lack of balance in our world does us all harm. Men are lonely, isolated, and overly aggressive and competitive with one another. Our world is not a warm and secure place, and I think that's because women are not there in partnership with men.

What's happened with equal opportunity, which I passionately disagree with, is that we've set up a competition. I think it's done more harm than good. The institutionalised side of affirmative action has done a lot of harm, and it has caused resentment in organisations. Telstra did a huge study and I was involved with quite a large number of the women. Even though 70 per cent of their intake are women, only 42 per cent of their middle managers, 12 per cent of their senior managers and only 0.5 of their top managers are women. What happens along the way? The men turn around and say, well, women get more opportunities in this organisation than we do. But when you look behind the scenes, they're not. Equal opportunity has created an illusion around it and I think it's set up resentment. There's a massive exodus of senior women. It's not what they want, but the positive side is that they're also fuelling an entrepreneurial evolution. Seventy per cent of the new business start-ups are women and they've got something like a 70 per cent higher chance of success because they ask for help earlier. They engage people more. So we really are in the middle of an entrepreneurial revolution. There are more start-ups today than there have been in the last twenty years. It's huge. We've got this intellectual exodus from big organisations. Men are leaving as well because they're seeking a challenge. New cultures are being set up in entrepreneurial businesses. It's not just the product and the service they're developing, it's also the way they run their businesses. They're more enlightened. I like it. I rather fancy myself as Boadicea. For me, my most energised, invigorated, excited and happiest place is the prow of the ship on a stormy sea with a cutlass in my hand. The message is, don't take life too seriously, it's a swashbuckling adventure. I'd probably come back as a pirate if I had the chance. If somebody says you can't do that, I have an overwhelming desire to do it. I'd like you to like me but I don't care if you don't. For me it's not connected to my judgement of you.

I've decided to be a very eccentric old lady on a Harley Davidson with long red hair. I've always fancied having a motorbike and I've dreamed about having one for most of my life, except I've never got a licence. I'm sick of being caught in my dreams for driving a motor-bike without a licence, so it's time to do it. My approach to clothing is I have one person in my life who I want to look sexually attractive for and that's my partner, otherwise I want to neutralise it. I like to look attractive for myself but it's not a big deal. I like being fit, I like being physically strong. Being good-looking is not as important to me as being in a strong body. People can say you're a handsome woman, which always irritates me, because you immediately go, ah-hah, that's a euphemism for 'you're ugly'. A strong body is my ship and it carries this amazing heart and mind around and I want them to be cared for.

island holiday

*F*abian Dattner has perfected the art of never giving up. It's not simply dogged persistence. It involves having a basic belief that most people will help you if you ask in the right way, matched with an ability to learn from any experience. She is firm in her belief that if you really want something then you will find a way of achieving it.

Rejection is hard to learn how to deal with. So often we give up too soon because we are hurt or disappointed or just miffed.

I had really wanted the author Colleen McCullough to be a chapter in my book Tall Poppies Too *and she had agreed, providing I came to Norfolk Island where she lived.*

I had done a special deal with my travel agent for a fare and accommodation which was non-negotiable. For once I had planned ahead and everything was organised. Then a week before I was due to leave a letter arrived from her secretary cancelling the interview and informing me that she would be busy writing for the rest of the year. Perhaps I could reschedule for the following year? Not likely. I was already three months behind on my deadline. It had to be now. Or never.

With the lessons that Fabian had taught me from her own experiences and after a hearty lunch (surprise, surprise) with my friends, I decided for the first time in my professional life, not to take 'No' for an answer.

I grabbed my passport, caught the next plane from Sydney to Norfolk Island, checked into the hotel and hired a car. There was, however, one tiny problem. I didn't know where she lived. The only address I had was a post office box. The islanders were very protective of her security. I had to be careful because the travel agent had done the deal on the basis of my interview with Ms McCullough and I didn't want to drop her in it. All I had been able to slyly ascertain from the person on the hotel desk was that there were a lot of bunya palms around the homestead. As I hit the roads I realised that the whole island is covered with bunyas.

Coast to jagged coast.

Up and down, around and around the dirt roads, I tore along in the little car, trying hard not to skittle cows, which are allowed to roam freely, and octogenarians in matching tracksuits and giant Reebocks. They clearly breed them on the island too.

When a car suddenly screeched to a stop at a crossroads, so did I. Clambering out, I explained that I was supposed to be at Colleen's house for an interview but I was lost. The driver gave me a complicated list of directions that I tried desperately to memorise. After more ups and downs and twists and turns, I found myself in front of a property that had huge palms running either side of the main path leading towards a house with a large wooden verandah. This was it. I stepped out of the car and approached the front step. A five-foot-tall carving of a woman with big tits, big smile, arms outstretched, greeted me. Had to be her house. Carved into the wooden stand was the word 'welcome'. A promising sign. Two large tables covered with tablecloths held down by cups full of teaspoons sat under the eaves of the verandah. She clearly entertained here a lot. I could see us sipping endless cups of tea, chatting away, her hearty laugh ringing through the bunyas.

I knocked on the door.

Silence.

I knocked again. Loudly.

Nothing was stirring, not even a mouse.

I peered through the window. All I could see was a piano. And bare boards.

As I walked back towards the car I decided it was the wrong house. Not grand enough.

Too folksy.

Back on the trail, I stared at the tourist map and kept driving. I swept past an unprepossessing gate that led into a long drive with rows and rows of palms. I kept going. Huge Moreton Bay fig trees with feet like dinosaurs loomed over the road. I kept driving. The road stopped at the crest of the hill. Beneath me was the Pacific Ocean, gnashing its teeth on foaming black rocks. As far as my eyes could see, it stretched.

As huge as the sky above. And as clear. How easy it would have been to simply metamorphose here in the afternoon sun and let it all wash over me. If I closed my eyes I could easily have nodded off. I forced myself to start the engine. Slowly I turned the little car around and drove back past the Moreton Bay figs, to the inconspicuous driveway. Cautiously I edged up the road and followed it until it turned into a large expanse of lawn. On my left was a very high hedge. There was a car parked on the grass near a pathway that led to a huge white house. I kept following the road, which went to the end of the hedge and stopped at a shed. Containing two blokes. I stepped out of the car and said, 'Hi'. One of them smiled and said, 'Can I help you?'

'I'm looking for Colleen McCullough,' I said, with more confidence than I felt.

'Is she expecting you?' he said. Politely, with no trace of cynicism or disbelief.

'Well, sort of,' I said. 'I have a letter here.' I tugged frantically at the envelope in my pocket.

'Name?' he said, pulling a phone from the wall. He talked quietly into it. I could hear my name being mentioned.

'Ric says he'll be out shortly.'

'Fine.'

It was only a few minutes before I saw a tall sturdy man striding purposefully towards me. As he came closer, I could see he was frowning.

'You must be Ric,' I said, walking towards him, my hand outstretched. He shook it warmly, but still frowning, said, 'I'm sorry but I thought you were told that it wasn't convenient for you to see Colleen this weekend.'

'Yes, well, I was. But, well, you see, I have this letter.' I grabbed the letter out of my pocket and thrust it towards him like a pensioner with a concession card.

He read the letter. He was still frowning. 'When did you arrive?'

'This afternoon. I had already booked my ticket and, well, it was the kind you can't refund.'

'Colleen's publishers from England were on your plane. They have just arrived and she will be tied up discussing business the whole weekend. Didn't her secretary tell you this?'

'She said that Colleen was so busy that it had to be next year and I couldn't believe that Colleen wouldn't understand my publishing deadline if I came here. I couldn't believe she was someone who would break her word when it had been arranged for so long, and if I just came over here . . .'

I was drowning in a sea of words. A sea bigger than the Pacific. He was shaking his head and staring at his boots.

'I'm sorry but it's just not possible . . . When are you leaving?'

'Tomorrow's plane, 3.10 I think. But I'll rearrange everything and stay longer if necessary.'

He shook his head. I looked imploringly into his eyes. They were kind eyes.

'I'll speak to Colleen but I really doubt it.'

He was starting to walk away from me. I ran to the car and grabbed *The Matriarchs*, one of my books, from my bag. I thrust it towards him. 'I brought this for her.'

He smiled and took it graciously. He looked at the cover and held the book with care. His hands were large but gentle. I liked him. She was lucky.

Bloody lucky.

'We have a friend who knows of your work.'

'Please, if you could plead my case. I only need an hour. I'll come at 6 am or 10 pm. Whenever it suits her.'

'Where are you staying?'

I babbled out the name of the hotel and my room number.

'I'll see what I can do. But I wouldn't hold out much hope. I'll ring you in the morning.'

I had to stop myself from kissing those large hands.

'Thank you, thank you. I really appreciate it.'

'Bye,' he said, turning away from me and walking towards the men in the shed, who had been talking among themselves.

'Bye,' I said, getting into my car and backing down the drive. My heart was heavy. I didn't think she was going to give in. But he did say he would try.

What a nice bloke. And so good-looking. The sort of looks you can trust. I steered back past the car still parked on the grass. English bloody publishers. I remembered seeing a young, very English-looking chap in the airport while we were waiting to go through customs. Shock of brown hair, cherry-red lips, summer clothes out of season, pale skin. I thought he looked like the Pom character in Tom Wolfe's *Bonfire of the Vanities*. Charming, urbane, into every freebie imaginable. Including, it seemed, a trip to Norfolk Island. I drove slowly past the serried palms and out on to what passed for a main road.

I was sick of all the green pastures and the fat cows. I had a headache and a stomachache. I returned to what was laughingly called my Superior Suite. It smelled worse than I remembered. I took two painkillers and climbed fully clothed into bed. When I woke up it was nearly dark. Where was I? And what was that smell? Dark, dank death. Someone in a brightly coloured tracksuit and new sneakers had died in here. I ransacked the wardrobe. I was going balmy.

I went to the reception desk. 'Could I please make a phone call to Sydney?'

The girl, wearing the expression of a professional mourner, looked at her watch and drawled, 'Switch closes at six.'

I said, 'But it's only five to six.'

She said, 'I'll try. If it comes though, it will be in the foyer out there. Do you want it charged to your room?'

'Yes, please.'

At one minute to six the phone in the empty foyer rang. I picked up the receiver. A female voice said, 'Your call's coming through.'

In my ear the phone rang and rang and rang and finally a cheery voice that I suddenly recognised as my own said, 'I'm sorry we can't take your call but if you'd like to leave a message.'

After the interminable pips I muttered, 'I have to be quick. Switch closes at six. I wasn't successful today but the husband is ringing tomorrow. Bye.'

The manger of the hotel walked past me. 'Everything okay?'

'Fine, thank you,' I said. Toothy smile.

'Do I have to book for dinner?' I asked the girl on the desk.

'I'll do it. Just for one, is it?'

'Yes,' I said, feeling like an abandoned, middle-aged spinster.

'Too bad you're not staying on. It's dress-up tomorrow night. Music hall.'

No doubt she thought I might get lucky—I might nab a geriatric widower. We could honeymoon here in our matching tracksuits and play sneaker tootsies under the table.

The dining room was straight out of a music hall. Red tablecloths, red velvet chairs, red candles. Five couples were seated around the edge of the dance floor. It had a scroll overhead that read 'Old Time Varieties'. Oh, please.

I sat down next to a couple whose heads were in their soup bowls.

Finishing first, she said, 'There's that couple who were on our bus trip today. I'll just go over and say hello.'

Without looking up he replied, 'Don't be long. Main course will be here soon.'

She crossed the dance floor and stopped at the table of a man who had been talking loudly to his wife and flirting with the waitress.

'Do you know I spent $950 on her today,' he said. Red-faced, strawberry nosed, slicked-down hair, a cigarette never out of his hand, he didn't wait for a response.

'The Pringle shop. Shirt, jacket, bag and scarf.'

'No shoes?' said the visiting woman.

'Oh no,' said his wife, 'I've got to wear special shoes. I'll show you.' She bent down, pulled up the leg of her slacks, whipped off her short stockings and extended her foot. The other woman bent down to get a better look.

'One of my legs is half an inch shorter than the other. I used to fall over a lot.'

'So did I,' chimed in her husband. 'But I was usually pissed.' Loud laugh. Hacking cough. 'No point in having wealth unless you've got your health,' he said.

'They go together,' said the visiting woman.

'No, health comes first,' said his wife.

The main course arrived at the visiting woman's table. Her husband waved his table napkin at her and she returned to her seat.

'What did you find out?' said her husband.

'He's a drunk. And she's got plastic feet.'

'What?'

He stopped eating.

'I thought she was kidding too, but she showed me the scars.'

They finished their roast beef without further conversation.

Later, at the bar, I sat near Redface. His wife with the plastic feet was in the Ladies. He was leering at the waitress like a shark.

'She's a good one, this one. Aren't cha, darlin'? Meeting me later?'

'Never know your luck.'

'You'd get a shock with me, darlin'.'

'I'm a single girl. You'd better watch out.'

He decided it was time to show the waitress his scars. 'Slit from here to here.'

'So you've got an extra pocket, eh,' said the waitress.

'Yeah, with a zip on it so the scotchman can't get it.'

Another man joined him at the bar. His wife joined another wife at a table.

The shark shouted the other man a drink and began to recite, 'Here's to the girl with the golden shoes, she eats your food and drinks your booze, and then goes home to her mother to snooze. Stingy bastard.'

Loud laugh. Hacking cough.

The two of them propped up the bar, cigarette in one hand, drink in the other. The two wives at the table discussed Weight Watchers and the difficulty of sleeping in a strange bed.

The shark said to the waitress, 'Same again for the blokes.'

While she was refilling the beer glasses he said to anyone within earshot, 'Fifty years a member of the bowling club. Never had a bowling ball in me hand. Joined when I was nineteen.'

Above their heads in the bar, on the TV appeared the face of a writer called P. J. O'Rourke who said he had just written a book called *Holidays in Hell*. He was a tourist who only visited trouble spots. Places like Belfast, Beirut. I must get him to put Norfolk Island on his list, I thought grimly.

Shark was telling a dirty joke when one of the other wives said the bus had arrived to pick them up. Shark's face was now the colour of an overripe plum.

As they stumbled out of the bar, P. J O'Rourke said to the interviewer, 'Leisure in the west is obscene. Busloads of people drinking funny drinks with little umbrellas on top. Leisure is the new problem in the west. How to fill the time.'

How indeed. I returned to the room smelling of death and fell into the black hole of sleep.

At ten o'clock the next morning I was woken by a loud knock on the door.

'Phone call for you.'

I threw on a robe and raced along the corridor into the foyer.

The manager pointed at the phone.

I picked it up.

'Ric here.'

'Yes, Ric,' I said, trying to keep the panic out of my voice.

'I'm sorry, but Colleen says she just hasn't got the time to talk to you.'

Not wanting to give too much away in front of the manager, who was pointedly listening, I said, 'What if I stay until Monday?'

There was silence and a deep breath at the end of the phone.

I said nothing.

'I'll try. But Colleen said you have wasted your time coming here.'

'Thank you so much, Ric. I do appreciate it. Ring me tomorrow, okay?'

'Okay. But like I said, don't get your hopes up.'

'Thank you, Ric. Bye.'

I turned to the manager. 'I'll need to book in until Monday, if that's all right. The interview with Colleen is taking longer than I thought.'

'She's a clever lady, that one,' he said.

'She certainly is,' I replied, scampering back to my room. I didn't leave my room again until the following morning when Ric phoned to see if 9 am on Monday was all right.

He said I shouldn't overstay my welcome.

I loved that man.

Given the circumstances, Colleen was gracious and generous. What she told me you can read in her chapter in *Tall Poppies Too*.

As if being punished for my success, I was forced to stay on Norfolk Island three more days, due to a pilot's strike. No lunches or dinners for me in the dining room. Just room service. My only book was the collected works of the detective writer Raymond Chandler, which a friend had thrust into my bag before I left. Just in case. Not only did I discover the joy of reading Chandler but lying in bed with books is one of my favourite things in all the world. Those three days were bliss. Whenever I think of Norfolk Island, murder is never far from my mind. I never did find the dead body which I suspected was the cause of the strange smell in the room but I discovered that Fabian Dattner was absolutely right. Once you refuse to let rejection or failure deflect you from your purpose, the word 'no' loses a great deal of its power.

ANNE SUMMERS
Journalist and writer

Traditional Catholic upbringing in Adelaide. Oldest and only daughter, with five brothers. Early rejection by her father caused her great pain and conflict, which was only resolved years later when her youngest brother died of cancer. Despite winning a scholarship to university, she left school at sixteen to do clerical jobs in banks and offices. Always believed she was unattractive. Had an early goal to write a great book in order to leave her mark on the world.

Usually does the opposite from what she is told. Studied politics rather than English. Married fellow student and lived with him in an Aboriginal settlement where he was an arts and crafts officer. Returned to Adelaide to do honours degree, became caught up in the excitement of the sexual revolution, the student revolution and women's liberation. Marriage over, she moved to Sydney where she wrote her first book, *Damned Whores and God's Police*, and became a journalist. Has chosen not to have children, and has not regretted it. Is a risk-taker and sees life as an adventure. Became Women's Adviser to Prime Minister Hawke, then moved to New York as North American manager for Fairfax. Then raised enough money to buy the magazines *Ms* and *Sassy*. Forced to sell them because of advertiser boycott. Began a live-in relationship with an American who is nineteen years younger than her. Wants to have an interesting life and do things she finds challenging and rewarding.

Potts Point, Sydney

It was another bleak, wintry day, the kind of day that spreads gloom and despair. I knocked on the door of the terrace house in Potts Point that Anne had bought when she and her American partner, Chip, returned to Sydney to live and work. The face that greeted me was anything but gloomy. This was a woman happy with her life. I had seen her when she was at the peak of her excitement in New York and later in Adelaide after the wheels had fallen off her attempt to take the magazine world by storm. This was a different face. Very different. No make-up. No glasses. I had never seen her without her glasses. Should I mention it? I wondered. No. Don't start off by talking about appearances. Wait for her to talk about it.

She sat me down at a table in the dining room that overlooked the galley kitchen where she made us a cup of tea. She was in jeans and a sweater, the uniform of the full-time writer. The biographer Michael Holroyd once said he did all his writing in bed, but I find it too hard to really get comfortable to write in bed, though I love never getting out of my jammies. Or if I think someone might drop in, I'll don my tracksuit. No bra, no shoes, just lovely, loose, soft cotton. Bliss. (Not like Maggie Tabberer, who despairs of me 'letting my standards slip'. I tell her that the standards to which she refers are hers, not mine. She wrote her entire autobiography in full make-up and beautifully pressed and colour-coordinated clothes. Ah well, whatever gets you in the mood. It's hard enough for me to get down to hard work at any time, built as I am for leisure and pleasure.)

Anne's a worker. She says she loves getting up early and planning her day, she loves her study, and being a full-time writer has been one of her lifelong dreams. She's a cool customer. I never really know what she is thinking behind all those words that come so smoothly out of her mouth. It's hard to throw her off her pitch. As a journalist she knows all the tricks.

All that early rejection from her father means that she looks to no one for approval. Or does she? 'What about male mentors?' I asked. She listed a few.

'And what about having affairs with powerful men?' Had she written about that in the autobiography she was working on?

There was a definite intake of breath. Perhaps even a bridling at my question. 'I'm not up to that part of the book.'

I could have pursued it but decided against it. I didn't want her to think that I was into some kind of lurid exposé, because I wasn't.

When it was time to go I said thank you and kissed her on the cheek. Not that I go around kissing people a lot. Rarely, in fact. But when you've been engaged in an intimate conversation about someone's life, especially if it's someone you already know, it seems, well, appropriate. She stood at the door watching as I opened the door of my vintage Mercedes sportscar.

I turned to look at her, smiling. 'It's a working-class girl's dream, isn't it?' I called out.

She laughed and nodded her head. As I surged away from the kerb, the wind whipped up old newspapers that flew past the windscreen and obscured my view. I slowed down. On days like this, I thought, you can't afford to take your destiny for granted.

In New York I was still under contract to the people who bought *Ms* but they wouldn't give me a job. So I was in a fairly unpleasant limbo where I was still getting a good salary but I didn't have any work to do. It was a very difficult time and very hard to know how to handle a situation like that. If I'd gone out and got a job I would have presumably suffered a huge drop in income. Because I had a five-year contract, when I bought my apartment in New York I signed a special five-year mortgage where I paid the same amount regardless of what happened to interest rates, and this deal was struck at a time when interest rates were very high and so my payments on my apartment were very, very high because I presumed I had security of tenure for five years. Silly me. But it did mean that after I'd lost my job I was trying to do various bits of freelance writing and various other things, and was succeeding to some extent, but American newspaper journalism pays next to nothing and there's no way in the world I could have supported myself on that. So I didn't try to get a new full-time job, which possibly was a mistake, but anyway I didn't.

That was why when Paul Keating approached me in early 1992 and asked if I'd come back just for a couple of months, to give some advice on communicating with women, I was able to do it because I had a lot of time on my hands. The only trouble was that when I did it, the guy who'd bought the magazines decided that it was a breach of contract and chopped me off. So I was stranded back here in Australia with no money and a big mortgage in New York to support. I was really supposed to stay with Keating for only three months but I ended up staying there for eleven months, up until the March 1993 election. Much to my surprise I found that Australia had changed in all sorts of good and interesting ways. I thought it was a terrific place and I particularly got caught up in the optimism, the way in which the arts community seemed to be so adventurous and forward looking.

One very important moment for me was the Arts for Labor function at the State Theatre that was organised two weeks before the election. The arts community basically showcased its talent as a means of thanking Keating for his support and it occurred during a very low point in the campaign, when he was very demoralised and depressed and didn't think he could get through the afternoon, let alone the campaign. The whole performance that day had such an incredible impact on him. It really boosted him. He was a changed man. I remember standing at the back of the State Theatre in Market Street, watching these performances and thinking, This is incredible, this country is fantastic, and I just thought, Okay, I'm going to come back.

Of course, I didn't know that within three years it was all going to change for the worse. So I came back at a time of great optimism and I was offered the job of editor of *Good Weekend*. It seemed to me that maybe another magazine job would be good, especially one that had such a huge circulation—it goes to about two and a half million readers a week. In retrospect I stayed too long. It's the sort of job I probably should have done for two years rather than four. When I did resign, everyone assumed I must have been fired because no one

resigns from jobs that not only give you great influence but unbelievable perks. You get invited to everything that's going, every party
in town, and I had a good salary, but at the end of the day you think,
This is not enough for me. The free tickets are all very well but you
pay in other ways.

I had been thinking for some years about giving it all up and taking
up full-time writing. My 52nd birthday was coming up and I said to
myself, well, what are you waiting for? What is the big occasion that's
going to make you decide now is the time to do it? So I just thought,
Okay, fuck it, and I made the decision on the Saturday. The following
Friday I left. And I am so pleased I did.

I put out a three-book proposal to the industry and in the end I
had three publishers bidding for it. I hired a very good entertainment
lawyer and he basically conducted the deal.

I don't miss the buzz of the office. Maybe I'm a bit anti-social.
I reckon the opera does one or two good ones a year and I try and go
to those and I pay for my own tickets. I still go to some of the parties
but I'm just less interested in that kind of social existence, as I don't
have to do it for work any more. I love being at home. Chip and I
spend a lot of time here. He goes to university most days. But it is a
very different way of living. It's what I've wanted for a long time. We
have separate offices. If he's not here I wouldn't stop for lunch, but if
he's here, well, we'll just grab something. We often go for a walk to
get out of the house, get a bit of fresh air, and it's nice to have the
harbour so close. During the summer we get up very early in the
morning and walk down to the pool, swim, walk. It's a different sort
of life but it's one that I really have wanted for a very long time.

I had hoped that we could do a lot more travelling than we're doing,
but now that Chip's going off to China for a year, I'll probably do a
bit of travelling on my own. I would love to be able to figure it out so
that we could go to New York for a couple of months of the year. We're
probably the first generation of women who in their fifties still see lots
of adventures ahead and feel that life's not over, thank God. I'm not
saying it was so for our mothers, but it was much more difficult for

them because they had kids and a lot of them were grandmothers by the time they were in their fifties. I have lots of friends in their fifties who have children and they're still having great lives and they're still creating adventures for themselves. I'm not saying it's not possible but there's just a whole different set of responsibilities and duties. If I had them my life would be different and I'm sure it would be wonderful, but I don't have kids. And I don't regret that.

The issues in my autobiography are more about growing up in a puritanical Catholic environment where we were taught that sex outside marriage was a mortal sin. I wanted to describe what it was like, to have that kind of basis for your education and then to go headlong into the sixties and then go into the women's movement, where everything was put on its head. Sex hasn't been a great force in my life. It's different at different times of your life, depending on who you're with and how you feel. When you've lived through very tumultuous political times as I have, and going through some of the women's movement stuff, there was a whole period of radical celibacy where some of us decided that we couldn't really deal with men.

I've had what these days are called mentors and most of mine have been men. That, to a large extent, reflected the fact that the men had all those jobs in those days. It was a man who was the head of Penguin, it was a man who was editor of the *National Times*, it was a man who was running the government department at Sydney University. A lot of those people who really were good to me and helped me were men. One of the things that I think I got out of having a difficult relationship with my father was that at the end of the day I don't give a fuck what people think of me. I don't need approval as a way of either motivating myself or keeping me going. I think that's been something which has been very useful, and if you can survive on people's disapproval or even on their dislike, that puts you streets ahead these days.

I had some very major punches while at Fairfax. The reason I stayed there as long as I did was because I wasn't going to leave while people were trying to get rid of me. There were certain people who were determined to get rid of me, and I refused to be forced out merely to satisfy the whims of certain individuals. I decided I would go when I was good and ready and not when I was being pushed. Being accused of sexual harassment was horrible. I think I know why they did it, and I think I know who did it but it's very hard to pin these things down.

There are two things about it that I found very interesting. How they get used in my life, who knows, but they're there. One is the length certain people will go to to achieve their ends—the extent of pure evil among certain people is just astonishing. Most of the time, most people are pretty decent and most people are reasonably easy-going, particularly in this country. So you're not often confronted with something as malevolent as that was. The second thing is that I was just absolutely staggered by the number of people who got in touch with me, who rang me or sent flowers or letters or telegrams or whatever, people who I didn't know, who said, 'Look, we know what's happening, don't let them get to you.' A lot of them were people who had been subject to public pillory themselves.

What was really horrible is that I didn't even know about it for at least a week after the whole of Australia was talking about it. I knew nothing until a friend of mine rang up and said, 'Do you realise that people are saying that sexual harassment charges are being laid against you?' I said, 'Well, that's just complete rubbish, I don't know what you're talking about. As usual the journalists have got it wrong.' In fact we did have an internal staff situation at *Good Weekend*, where one staff member had complained of harassment, not sexual harassment but harassment, from another staff member and formally complained to me and I was being forced to deal with it. It was an extremely unpleasant situation but it was nothing to do with sex. I assumed that that's what they were talking about.

Within a day of that, the *Courier Mail* wrote this story where they named me and headlines said 'Summers Accused Of Sexual Harassment', or something. After a lot of legal advice I decided to fight back, writing an article myself. It carried its risks. Once I had written that, it just opened the floodgates. I still think that I had to do it because there was no other way of dealing with the rumours. I had to fight them. It was all round Australia. I had people ringing me from everywhere. How do you sue individuals? How do you prove it? I didn't sue them because I don't believe journalists should sue, but I certainly got them to publish my version of events. I was extremely distressed by the whole thing and it was very, very tough for both of us. Chip was incredibly supportive but he was incredibly frustrated about not being able to actually do anything practical to help. He's fantastic. He's great in terms of talking about tactics and how to handle things. It was horrible because you just never knew what each day was going to bring. There were lots of different twists and turns. It went on and on because then the Journalists Union declared me black, my staff weren't allowed to speak to me, and that went on for about a month.

I lasted about two years in the job after that. Most people roll over, and I wasn't going to do that. It toughens you up. I don't see the world as a school but you do try not to repeat your mistakes. There are certain people, and I guess they're mostly men, though there are some women as well, who have no other big interests in life but to play the game of exercising power within their work environment. I'm not interested in doing that. I was determined to protect myself and not be squashed like a bug, but at the end of the day what I want to do in my life is not to win some bloody corporate battle when, three weeks later, no one can even remember what it's about. They're not going to crush me. It's a belief in myself. I know I'm strong, I know I'm brave, I know I'm not going to be ground down, and I will keep going.

I am currently extremely angry at the hypocrisy of some men in the Labor Party who say that childcare is welfare but that tax deductions for plumbers' tools or electricians' things or businessmen's libraries or whatever is a legitimate tax expense. It's always been a problem in the Labor Party and that's why Keating was so remarkable and so was Hawke, in that they both agreed at critical times in history on the importance of childcare for women as a means of giving women with kids the freedom to make choices. But there are also so many people in the Labor Party who understand the importance of childcare and that's why they're against it because deep down they do not want women out of the home. For example, the battles we had with Peter Walsh about childcare during the Hawke government were legendary. They were just shocking. What distresses me is that this whole new generation of younger men, who all have working wives, who all have daughters, who you would hope might be a little more reconstructed, they're suddenly coming out with all these archaic attitudes. Childcare is the absolute linchpin issue. I'm not talking about millionaires or even high salaries. I'm talking about a combined family income of less than $40 000.

I find the whole way in which you achieve things through politics really interesting. I've been in and out of it a lot and I'm not saying I would never go back into it but I think it's unlikely. I've moved past that.

I've always been very blunt in my language, but that's the way to get people to take notice of you. If you just pussy-foot around, people can first of all avoid the message or misconstrue it, or they can not bother about responding to it. So that's always been my style, to be upfront.

I plan to support myself by writing. I hope that I never need to take another job. I do most of my chatting by e-mail. I'm very happy.

Persistence is certainly one of my strongest qualities. It's probably less important now because I'm not trying to elbow my way in anywhere that's trying to stop me, but there have been times in the past when that's been important.

Writing an autobiography meant that I had to look at my early schoolday photos. I always believed that I was big and fat and when I went back through all the old school magazines I saw this thin little thing. I thought, That can't be me. All my perceptions were coloured by that fact that I was unhappy, that's my memory. My mother disputes that. But when I go back and try and remember stuff, I remember the unhappy bits more than the other bits, which is perhaps unfair but who can help what the memory does? I don't think there's such a thing as an inner child. That's just psychocrap. I'm not interested in that.

One of the things you try and work out about yourself when you write about your life is, how did I become who I am?

There was a competition I got into in, of all places, a 'five-stars club' in the *Southern Cross* newspaper in Adelaide when I was about ten. It became a frenzied competition with another girl to be the first one to win a particular prize. I am amazed when I go back and read all these letters about what I used to do, every week sending in short stories and articles and jokes and poems and riddles. I didn't win, I came second. This has happened to me a lot in life, coming second. I got second-class honours in my degree and that was devastating. Anyway, I went into a huge sulk when I was a kid about this *Southern Cross* thing. The guy who ran the page publicly taunted me about not stopping just because this other girl had beaten me. He made me finish and that was horrible. The competition went on for about two years. I was twelve. Then I found out that she was sixteen. What's a sixteen-year-old doing, hanging out in the kids' pages of a Catholic newspaper? So that made me feel a lot better. I have a huge competitive streak, and because I never played sport I guess it came out in this literary competition.

I'm still concerned with how I look, not that I'm doing much about it these days because one of the bad things about sitting at my desk eight hours a day is that my big diversion is I cook and I eat and drink much more than I probably should. I'd like to lose a bit of weight. I recently had laser surgery on my eyes so I don't wear glasses any more, so that's a big change. It's fantastic. I've worn glasses since I was five. This wasn't cosmetic, this was so I could see better, and it's worked brilliantly. Real cosmetic surgery I'm not against, but I probably won't do it.

I still don't really think that I'm old. I don't feel old. I just don't think it's an issue, the nineteen-year difference between Chip and me. I know that it will become one—the body starts to give up on you—but I hope that in keeping the reasonably fit lifestyle we have that I can put it off for a bit longer. A lot of people criticised me for having the laser surgery and said, 'Oh, you're mad, you're losing your signature look.' I said, 'You wouldn't say that to a cripple who got rid of their crutches, would you?' I did wonder how I'd feel when I'd had something between me and the world all my life. That feeling of being naked lasted about three days and now I look at photographs of myself with glasses and think, God, I look strange. It's incredible how quickly I've adapted to it and I just think it's fantastic. My vision is better now than it was with glasses so I'm better off. I'd been thinking about it for over two years. I had a little special bank account so I set the money aside.

I now manage all our investments, our super fund. I actually spend quite a lot of time on financial matters and I have become quite good at it. The bit that I'm not good at is controlling my own spending. I still have a lashout. I buy couturier clothes and we spend an unbelievable amount on food. We don't go out a huge amount. It's very easy to spend money in this town. It's nice to have money and not to have to worry about it, but I'm not somebody that wants to be out there. If somehow we won Lotto and had 20 million dollars I don't think that would be great. You could have a quarter of what we've got and be better off if you were more frugal than we are, or you could have ten times as much as we've got and be broke all the time. Chip's got various part-time jobs.

Chip and I have a very good relationship. It's not unstable but we do fight a lot. But that's healthy. A lot of our friends hate it. We try not to fight in front of people but sometimes do. We both say what we think. We've been together for just over ten years now. It's the longest relationship of either of our lives. He's happy. He recently became a citizen and so he's made a commitment to Australia. He's a dual citizen, so I would still hope we can move between the two countries, but who knows? The thing that characterises our relationship is that he's willing to take me on, and does, on all sorts of things. He's not afraid to say whatever he wants to me. If he thinks I'm bullshitting, he tells me, and I'm a big bullshitter. I just like telling stories. He's a great bullshit detector. We now know each other so well—there's not many tricks you can pull on someone when you've been together for that long. He has a lot of areas in his life that I don't share. He's going to China for a year on a scholarship. He's very involved in music, he sings with the Philharmonia—he spends a huge amount of time with that.

Life is still an adventure. I usually have two or three things going at any one time. I usually just lie in bed for a few minutes in the morning and plan what I'm going to do. I never ever turn the television on in the daytime. I can't remember the last time I went to a drinking lunch. I'm not saying I'm against it, it just hasn't happened for a while. I actually prefer dinners.

I'm not as optimistic about the future of women as I would have been two years ago. Only because I've seen with alarm the ways in which things that I thought were the new certainties are able to be, if not reversed, certainly undermined or weakened. I'm thinking in particular of policies like childcare and certain things that made it easier for women that have been under assault from all sides of politics. I had thought that women, once out of the cages, could never be locked up again. More and more women you hear saying, oh, it's all such a struggle and it's terrible and it's stressful and do we want to be like the men? I'm worried there's going to be a major revisionism and that maybe the girls that are two or three today will grow up wanting to be happy housewives. It's really important that women continue to get as much education as they possibly can because that's a gateway to everything else. There doesn't seem to be any sign that it's slackening off but I'm worried that it's only true for the really bright girls.

Maybe the future gap is not between girls and boys, or men and women, it's between educated people versus uneducated people. That would be also very distressing. The gap between the rich and the poor has already happened to a pretty alarming degree. I'd be very happy to be proven wrong. But I look at what's happened in the past and I remember reading all about that time after the Second World War when women were forced back into the home. When we were discovering all this stuff back in the seventies, we said, 'Oh good God, that could never happen again because we're all too smart and we wouldn't want to go back to the home.' Of course, we as individuals wouldn't but that's not to say that another generation won't look at their stressed-out mothers or grandmothers and say, 'I don't want to live like that.'

We have to learn from history and history tells us that there have been a number of periods in the past where in fact things have been reversed. I was interviewed by my nine-year-old niece the other day for her school project and she asked, 'Anne, why did you become a feminist?' How do you explain that to a nine-year-old in three sentences? That was quite a challenge. I said, 'Well, when I was growing up, girls didn't get the same money for doing the same jobs that boys got.' She didn't react either way, she just wrote it all down as I told her. Hers is the generation to watch, to see what they do. I am a bit pessimistic, partly because I've seen the sort of viciousness of the political backlash in this country. I think there's a deep-seated misogyny in the Labor Party.

Generally there's a bit of tokenism about sharing power with women—it's no more than lip service. The fact that it's now seen that there should be a certain number of women on most boards is seen as a concession. I honestly think that the fight by women to get on to boards is a totally misguided attempt and a total waste of time. If some individuals want to do it, fine, but to see that as women's main battle I think is wrong. Getting more women into politics is different, however, because that has far more influence. But the story of women in politics in Australia has been abysmal. Every woman who looks like getting somewhere is knocked down. Certain thresholds have been crossed and certain barriers have been lowered but we are still not even close to women being seen as a normal part of politics. We're certainly not close to the idea of women in real positions of power. A woman prime minister in this country is still a long way off. I can't see it in the foreseeable future.

funeral day

*B*oth Anne Summers and I are part of a long tradition of strong women born in Adelaide. South Australian women (excluding Aboriginal women) were the first women in Australia to gain the vote and the first women in the world to win the right to stand for parliament. During 1994 and the Centenary of Suffrage celebrations it was realised that most of us knew nothing about these pioneering women. Their public lives had been recorded, their private lives had not.

Dame Roma Mitchell was the first female governor of South Australia, the first female QC in Australia and the first woman to sit on the bench of the Supreme Court. When she died I decided to return home to Adelaide to attend her state funeral.

The morning was hot and sticky. (We still act as if we are not in the middle of Asia: no one had thought to install fans in the overcrowded cathedral.) I sat, in my hat, fanning myself with the programme like a Southern belle of a certain age. Together with all the other hundreds of people who had known and respected her, I listened to the eulogies. But they were all about her public life. What, I wondered, was the truth about her private life? Did she have a private life? Even her closest friends claimed they never knew. Over the years I had heard many theories about why she had never married and who she had loved.

In 1987, when I had interviewed her for my book *The Matriarchs*, I reminded her that in a recent newspaper article the journalist had inferred that her failure to marry was because a man she had loved had died in the war.

'He's quite wrong. Quite wrong. Certain things in my life are private and that's that.'

She proceeded to pour me a gin and tonic so strong that I could hardly speak.

Good tactic.

I had once spoken to a previous state premier about her private life and he'd said, 'Her secrets will die with her.' As indeed they have, unless correspondence comes to light and reveals a rich and full private life very different from her public image. But for someone who guarded her privacy so astutely in life, it is highly unlikely that she would not have planned to protect herself in death.

Once women came to the realisation that the personal was political, we knew it was essential that if we were to tell the truth about our lives, then the connection between the public and the private had to be revealed. Sex and sensuality are intrinsic to an understanding of anyone's life but have usually been hidden or ignored in the stories of the lives of great women. Our culture has always sought to hide the truth and contradictions of women's passions.

Women at the turn of this century, unlike the last, no longer have to hide their ambition or refuse the trappings of power. Some wear their power and ambition comfortably, like a velvet cloak around their shoulders. Others, however, have become crazed with it, obsessed by it. They secretly long to be modern-day Evitas, standing on a balcony with thousands of people calling out their name. They have opted to become slaves to the media and their own public relations machines. Anything justifies seeing their name in print or their face on television. Neither Anne Summers nor I have ever spoken the truth about these women. Why not? In the last twenty years there have been too many genuine misogynists, men and women, hungry for such information in order to destroy the small gains that have been made.

I thought all this while looking at the Adelaide women sitting upright in the wooden pews. They were all there. The good, the bad, the mad and the mediocre. Here in the driest state in the driest continent, the waters of freedom flowed freely in the late 1800s and then dried up. It wasn't until the 1970s that a stream half forgotten was tapped by the premier Don Dunstan, a stream that led the nation and flowed around the continent. Sitting in this holy place, with tears in their eyes for the passing of a great woman, these women wept also for the passing of a great era, the passing of a piece of history in which they had played a part.

When we all gathered outside the cathedral, we decided that the only way to truly celebrate the life of a great Adelaide woman was with lunch. Dame Roma had been known to enjoy an elegant lunch in this city that makes the best food and wine in the country. Sitting around the table I looked at the faces of these women, some well known, others not, who, like Dame Roma, had been part of Dunstan's era of change. Mary Beasley, who he appointed as the first Commissioner for Equal Opportunity, remembered the Melbourne Cup lunch she had shared with Dame Roma and other prominent women like Deborah McCulloch, who was the first women's advisor appointed by Dunstan. When it had begun to rain, Mary had raced out to put a big bet on a horse called Vanderhum. She remembered the genuine delight on Dame Roma's face when the horse won, and she joined in the celebration as Mary shouted bottles of French champagne. Mary continued for the next twenty years to ride in what became a steeplechase at the top of the Public Service. Like the best jockeys, whenever she fell, she picked herself up and got straight back on the horse. For her, tomorrow was always another race and another premier or another government.

At the end of the seventies, when idealism had become a dirty word and the chilly winds of the corporate eighties were blowing in, Deborah resigned to go to Paris with her lover and her son and write a novel about sex and power. In her stead she stepped 'the greed is good brigade', those who had been waiting for a chance to promote themselves. And they did, with the help of politicians who used them as Trojan horses. These women never rocked the ship of state. These women never challenged the hollow rhetoric and broken promises of both sides of politics. These women attached themselves to the powerful and the wealthy in order to promote themselves and their friends. All in the name of sisterhood.

This is not only an Adelaide story. It happened everywhere, especially Sydney, city of instant celebrity, where you can lay claim to anything as long as it makes good copy. Certain women . . . should I name them now that feminism is established as part of the fabric of our society and not so easy to damage? No, I think not. It would only give them cause for more press coverage. Anyway, these self-promoters continue to use the cause of women as a pathway to a career of celebrity speakerdom, board directorships and media recognition. They are very popular on boards because they never rock the boat. You will not find their names in any of my books. Much to their chagrin.

All popular movements attract those who seek to attach themselves purely for their own advancement but who are never there when the hard grassroots work has to be done. These stories of sex and power need to be told. Uncomfortable truths. Funerals remind you of the best and the worst in people.

I lifted my glass to toast Deborah McCulloch, who never finished her novel in Paris but returned home to continue her work for women. She now lives simply and quietly in Adelaide, continuing to help any woman in need. Her passion has never wavered.

After the service she introduced me to her child, now an adolescent, whom she has mothered and fathered, along with her one-time lover. They all live side by side, in adjoining cottages, their public and private lives linked for all to see. They are a family of the new millennium, forged from the social changes of the old. They all toasted each other, laughing and hugging, the women warriors. Those who had held the faith.

The midday sun belted down on those outside the cool restaurant. The merciless Australian sun. Bleaching lives and truths.

Who knows the history of how and why it all began in the 1970s? Who knows, the real stories of these warrior women and their lives and their passions? Certainly not the young women in the country who have benefited from their struggles and their passion. Every woman who gets a bank loan or a credit card, or who isn't sacked when she becomes pregnant or who wants to be an engineer or a plumber or prime minister, is indebted to them. Does it matter that they do not even know their names, let alone their stories? We did not know the names of the women whose struggles gained us the vote, not until feminism made us curious. I'm sure our daughters or granddaughters will discover the histories of the 1970s women when they are ready. The important thing is that their stories are written down. And that the truth is told.

Every woman should try at some stage of her life to tell her own story. Warts and all. Personal and public. It doesn't matter how well they write it, or if it is ever published, as long as it is the truth. Long after they have gone, their words and their truths will remain.

But what is the truth? Easy word to say. Whose truth are we talking about? Is non-fiction any more truthful than fiction?

Simone de Beauvoir, the woman who defined the terms of feminism in the last century, always kept a non-fiction journal, which she published as the true account of her life. She also wrote fiction. And yet when a woman threatened to come between her and her lifetime partner Jean Paul Sartre, in her journal she admitted to feeling no threat or jealousy. In the novel *She Came To Stay* she killed off the character who represents the woman with whom Sartre had become enmeshed. Which version gives the truth of her feelings?

Even my own descriptions of how I came to interview the women in my other books are not always strictly the truth. I have notebooks full of stories, which I believe will be better told under the cloak of fiction. Even in this book, where I am attempting to tell what I believe is the truth, the monologues I have constructed from the interviewee's versions of their lives are a distillation informed by my own views.

I asked these questions of myself and my companions over what became a very long lunch. It is a pity that we know nothing of Dame Roma's private life, only her public life. But then again, it's not every day that we get a chance to reflect on both the private and the public stories of our own lives. It takes a funeral, an ending, to remind us of the beginning of our awareness that the personal is always political.

SALLYANNE ATKINSON
Former lord mayor, company director

A peripatetic childhood until her parents settled in Queensland when she was twelve. Shy and underconfident as a child and adolescent, she was the oldest of four girls. She had a dominant mother, and married an equally dominant man, a neurosurgeon. She had four girls and a boy but never really liked the traditional role of mothering, even though she got on well with her children. She took up part-time journalism, her pre-marriage career, then worked part-time for a Liberal politician, after which time she was preselected as Liberal alderman and went on to be elected Lord Mayor of Brisbane.

A great believer in grabbing new opportunities, going to new places, meeting new people. She liked working in local government and being Lord Mayor because she gets great satisfaction from helping people in a practical sense. After the death of her mother, she separated from her husband of 25 years and moved into an apartment with her daughters. She was sick of being unhappy and was going through a period of re-evaluation and reassessment. After counselling, she decided to give her marriage another try. When she lost the next mayoral election she was stunned and at a loss. However, she is a great believer in fate, in destiny, and believes that everything happens for a purpose.

Ritz Carlton, Sydney

'Can we meet tonight?'

'Sure. But you sound terrible.'

'I've got a dreadful cough and cold and the doctor said I should be in bed.'

'Why aren't you?'

'It's too boring. Come in and we'll have room service for dinner.'

Room service, I'm ashamed to say, is one of my great weaknesses. Offer me room service in one of the best hotels and I'm anyone's. Well, practically anyone's. It remains my favourite luxury. Breakfast, lunch and dinner, preferably all three wheeled in on the trolley, eaten in bed or on the couch, is the best.

In as long as it took me to slap on the lippie, catch a cab and travel the eight minutes to the hotel, I was there, shiny eyed and bushy tailed.

'Good evening, madam, how lovely to see you again,' said the doorman who helped me out of the taxi.

'Thank you,' I said in my best broadcasting voice, thinking to myself, I've never been in this hotel in my life. Who does he think I am? I strode up to the reception desk and said, 'I have an appointment with Sallyanne Atkinson. Could you let her know I'm here.'

'Certainly', said the receptionist. 'Let me take you up to Mrs Atkinson's room.'

'On no, that's really not necessary,' I said.

'Not at all, ma'am. It's a pleasure,' she said coming out from behind the desk and smiling at me like it was indeed a pleasure.

Who do they think I am? I thought to myself as the lift glided to a halt and I followed her to the room.

'Have a pleasant evening, ma'am,' she said as Sallyanne opened the door to greet me.

'Are they always this nice to everyone?' I said, throwing myself into the plump cushions of the couch.

'Yes, they are extremely nice to me. Now, let's order. I'm starving. I'm having a hamburger and fries. Do you want to look at the menu?'

'That sounds great to me, but throw in a bottle of red as well.'

The wine duly selected, the order taken, we settled down with a gin and tonic to some serious gossip.

We had first met in a posh hotel. She was then in the full flush of being Brisbane's Lord Mayor and had been given a fabulous suite in the Adelaide Hyatt, where she was delivering a luncheon speech.

'I'll be with you in a minute. Have a look around,' she'd said. 'It's gorgeous. Wait till you see the bathroom. And the view from up here is amazing.'

Needing no further encouragement I took off on a detailed inspection, thinking, She is just as unaffected and natural as the media say she is. I tried hard to see whether this chatty, cheerful demeanour was merely a clever persona, but came to the conclusion that this woman had no artifice. In fact, I worried about some of the things she told me, which in the wrong hands could be used against her. Years later, when we had become good friends and I was staying with her in the embassy in Paris when she was Australian Trade Commissioner, I asked whether she had ever worried about her openness and honesty to me on that first meeting. She said, 'No, I decided that I could trust you, and I was right. I usually trust my instincts.'

The hamburgers and fries and red wine (mostly drunk by me, I have to confess) were accompanied by a very frank discussion of her life and her work as the Deputy Mayor of the Olympic Village. Most of what she told me was soon to emerge in the headlines of the daily newspapers that were tracking the debacles of the Olympic organising committee .

I could have stayed there half the night hearing all the inside stories but her coughing was taking its toll and eventually she gasped, 'I need to go to bed. I have a very early meeting in the morning.'

'What time?'

'Seven am at the Olympic Village, which means we will have to leave here at six.'

As if on cue the phone went and from the conversation I gathered it was one of her fellow board members asking her what time they should leave in the morning. If there is even one woman around, men will

inevitably give her the task of making the decisions over time of depar-
ture and organisation details. Nothing big, mind you, just the boring
mechanics of living which are either beneath them or beyond them.
Sallyanne slipped immediately into the role of helper and told him what
time to get up, what time to have breakfast and when to be in the foyer.
All she left out was when to go to the toilet.

'Don't go. You're really too ill to be trekking all the way out to Home-
bush,' I pleaded with her.

'Perhaps I will stay in bed tomorrow,' she said. 'I think I've worn myself
out tonight with all this talking.'

The doorman called me a cab and said, 'So nice to see you again,
ma'am'.

'Yes, lovely to see you,' I purred. It may have been a genuine mistake,
although I can't think of anyone famous who has the misfortune to look
like me, or it may have just been part of their 'charm the customer' routine.
Whatever the truth, it worked, and by the time I arrived home, I quite
believed I had been there many times. Or at least I wished I had.

The next morning when I rang Sallyanne to see how she was, I was
not surprised when the receptionist said, 'I'm afraid Mrs Atkinson's not
in her room. Would you like to leave a message?'

'No, thank you,' I said, thinking about her as a real trooper, sitting
around that table with all those men trying to ignore her, except when
her coughing drove them crazy.

I'm actually feeling good about myself at the moment. Nothing to do
with money. Very few people I know who are seriously rich are what
I'd call totally happy and fulfilled. They're often out of touch with
reality. It's all travel and glamour and clothes and lots of plastic surgery.

I've been through a pretty difficult period of my life personally and
professionally since being Lord Mayor of Brisbane. What you have to
keep saying to yourself about these bad patches is that they don't last

forever, even though sometimes it seems like they will. Most people have ups and downs in their lives and when you're on a down you have to just keep saying to yourself that you will get through it . . . eventually.

My marriage had been in trouble during my mayoralty. I never felt that Leigh, my husband, was on my side. I don't think that he ever really believed that I did the job of Lord Mayor, or even that I made the budget decisions. And yet the bizarre thing is that when he went to medical conferences, he would brag. Friends of mine would report back and say, 'He's so proud of you.' But whenever he went to public functions with me, he'd just sit there looking miserable. The good thing about him being a neurosurgeon was that I could always say, 'He's not here because he's operating in the morning.' When Fergie and Andrew were at a civic lunch and Leigh didn't come, the Duke of York said to me, 'I thought doctors could get people to cover for them.' I said, 'Well, you wouldn't like it if it was your head being operated on.' Anyway, Damien, my son, came instead and we all had a very nice time.

Basically, I don't think Leigh ever believed in me. We were never really friends. He wasn't a person I'd pour my heart out to or confide in. If you started to say, 'I feel really miserable,' he'd reply, 'What do you have to be miserable about?'

When I had lost City Hall, Leigh had said it was his turn to do what he wanted. It seems amazing when I look back on it. Anyhow, I said okay, and I thought I'd give it a go, being a supportive wife, which was an interesting time because apart from the fact that there really wasn't that much to do, I was there waiting with the dinner and he never came home. He would be operating or out at meetings. The Liberal Party had offered me a Senate seat and I had refused because of Leigh. If I had taken it, I would be in parliament still. It's interesting how these things happen. When I went through a low time when I was in Paris I thought, Oh my God, I've ruined my life.

So, anyway, I puddled around doing a few voluntary things and being the good wife. Leigh used to ask why I wasn't earning money.

But he didn't really want me to, I think. He really didn't know what he wanted. By 1992 I was starting to realise that this was not a good way to live. I remember him being in Korea at a medical conference, with me doing the conference wife, or the concubine, as a friend of mine used to refer to it, and talking to a Catholic priest there, who said, 'You've got to do what's right for you.' But by that stage all the Senate and Reps seats had gone. So misery, misery.

In that same year, when I went off to the Albertville Olympics, I met up with my daughter Nicola in Paris afterwards and she asked, 'How are you and Dad getting on?' And I said, 'Not well, I'm thinking about leaving him.' And then she told me that she was getting married. So I felt I couldn't leave then, with a wedding coming up. I filled my life with being busy. I was at that stage the Chairman of Sustainable Development Australia, which was ahead of its time but never got off the ground.

Six months before the election when John Hewson was the Opposition leader, the figures were looking winnable. I only needed a small swing to win the seat of Rankin. Everybody was saying, 'This is the unlosable election, the Liberals can't lose.' And I genuinely thought that those people in Rankin needed me. Interestingly, my son, who is a Labor supporter, and a really proper ideological one, said he wouldn't come and campaign with me because he didn't think that those people should have a Liberal representing them.

Leigh didn't want me to run. When I was going to the Olympics in Barcelona, I wrote him a letter saying that I was going to stand. He totally ignored it. He wouldn't even discuss it. I felt as if I was up against another brick wall. It's very hard to describe if you've never been in that situation. I'd told the party I was going to run. The morning of the preselection I felt Leigh didn't want me to win. But I did. I didn't, however, win the seat as the tide turned against Hewson and Keating won.

I finally made the decision to leave Leigh after the Christmas of 1993, when the children said the tension between us was unendurable. I decided to move in with my daughter Genevieve. As Leigh and I were both practising Catholics, all Leigh said when I left was that I would always be his wife.

In 1994 I was offered the Trade Commissioner's job for Austrade in Paris. I was trying to decide whether to take it, and one of the girls said, 'Listen Mum, how many women of your age get offered three years in Paris?'

By the time I landed at the embassy in Paris I hadn't had much time to think about what it was going to be like. The job was very isolated. The French, as a race, are not warm and welcoming and even though I had lots of friends there, it's a different kind of friendship from those friendships you take for granted. I learned an enormous amount about the things that matter in life and the things that you value and how important having a familiar framework and structure is. With the federal Labor government in power there was always that political thing, people being a bit suspicious about what I was doing there. I think Austrade was going through a phase where they wanted to bring people in from outside, and there weren't too many people in Australia with a French background. I had done French at university but I soon discovered how much I didn't know. I remember thinking before I went there that I would absorb all this French style and get thin, which didn't quite happen, but I think the pattern in my life is that every experience is a learning experience. It's another layer of learning, another layer of knowing more about things. So Paris was all those things.

It was the first time I'd ever been alone. I'd had five kids. I had grown up in a family with lots of people. Suddenly I was in this big apartment on my own. The others in the embassy were all proper Labor appointees. I was an outsider. I know there was a lot of resentment within the Labor party in Queensland about my appointment and a lot of protests.

I had been the only woman on the board of SOCOG (which I sat on for six months). The board meetings were okay but when we were away on visits the men just assumed that I'd want to go shopping with the wives. Before I was on SOCOG, I had been on the bidding committees for both Melbourne and Sydney because I knew all the members of the IOC from Brisbane's bid in 1986. That had been a very exciting time because we had never bid before and we cut across what people believed Australians to be—rough, sporty types. Here was this young woman as mayor and much was made of the French speaking. It was the old breath of fresh air stuff. So then, of course, they kept wheeling me out again and again.

In one sense I've never really been understood. I know that some of the Liberals from City Hall could never quite work out why I'd won the mayoralty. They were pleased that I had, because I brought them all in with me but, of course, after a few years they had forgotten that. They've never won since.

A common thread in my life is that I've always been an outsider. When I ran in the first place as an alderman they could never understand what I was doing there. The doctor's wife, the westerns suburbs housewife, why aren't you playing tennis? In Paris, I was always the Liberal even though I was appointed by the Labor Party. Again it was, What is she doing here?

I'm such an optimist that I always assume everyone's going to be nice and then I get a great shock when they're not. One of my basic tenets in bringing up the children was, always be nice to people and they'll like you better. By the end of my three years in Paris I'd made some very good friends, both here and in Paris, whom I still keep in touch with. The beginning was hard. But you just plough on. Soldier on and smile a lot. And learn to adjust to the circumstances. One of my daughters was carrying on one day about how, all my life, all I have done is accommodate other people. The girls were always saying to me with regards to their father, 'Stand up for yourself.' What they never really understood was that if you were an early sixties wife, like I was, the contract was that if you had dinner on the table at seven, they were nice to you. Young women today won't put up with that. The contract has changed and that's a good thing. It's true that I was the great accommodator. I was so busy trying to please Leigh, to please my parents, to please his parents, to please his older colleagues that I was forever juggling other people's needs. Women are great jugglers—it's expected of them. That's why they make good politicians if they're ever given the chance.

I suppose in a sense one of my failings as well as one of my strengths is that I never see the obstacles in front of me. I think, there's a mountain, let's go and climb it. I never think, oh gosh, this or that could go wrong. So I went to Paris without realising that I was putting together all of the greatest stresses that anyone could have. Leaving your marriage, starting a new job in a new country with no support structure. I survived. But I'm really glad that the nineties are behind me.

During my time in Paris, I always feared that I had made a mistake by being over there and not running for the federal seat of Rankin again. In the redistribution it had become a safe Liberal seat. I probably would have won preselection because I'd worked so hard in the electorate before. Some political analysts have even suggested that that was why Labor wanted me out of the country.

Last year, I made the huge decision to run for preselection in another seat and I failed to be selected. I found that very traumatic. Times and priorities have changed. It was so exciting to have a Liberal government in power and I felt like they were all having Christmas without me. Obviously it wasn't meant to be. I have always been a fatalist. In 1990 I was offered a federal seat. It was a last-minute thing, the guy was standing down and they had to preselect a candidate. To stand I would have had to leave City Hall and stop the things I was intent on doing, like finishing the Brisbane Plan. Of course, I often regretted not taking it, because I subsequently lost the mayoral election. The people didn't say thanks very much for hanging around and finishing your work. They said, 'Off.'

Who knows, perhaps I would have been a failure as a federal politician; perhaps I'd have hated it. The things I liked about local politics, like getting involved with people and helping them, I can do outside anyway and I do. I'm certainly over any regrets now. Fate or destiny probably did me a big favour. There's something very real and very satisfying about running a city and helping people, doing something to improve their lives. So much of the federal stuff is so juvenile. They remind me of kids sitting in their sandpits throwing sand at each other. I wonder now how much of my wanting to be part of that was other people's expectations. Was I just trying to please everyone again? Was I just going along with what the media and those in power expected me to do? Was it Sallyanne the great accommodator again?

Anyhow, so I came back from Paris, no home, no job, no partner. Leigh had remarried in the Anglican Church. I did find difficult the fact that the children, who are the most important things in my life, were spending half their lives getting to know him again. One part of me was delighted that they had a father and that they were behaving like mature and intelligent adults, and the other part of me wanted to yell out, 'I spent my life bringing you all up. I need your love and attention now more than ever.' I soldiered on as usual. I bought a traditional Queenslander house, which I'd always wanted to live in and Leigh hadn't, and I unpacked all my stuff. I was appointed to a couple of boards, one of which was the Chair of Queensland Tourism, which I loved. The only things I can ever really do well are things I actually believe in.

Eloise said I'm getting more and more eccentric. I said, 'What do you mean, more eccentric?' And she said, 'You mean you honestly don't think you're eccentric?' And I said, 'Oh, I've never really thought about it.' I've taken up Latin American dancing, which happens to be at West End, near where Eloise lives. I'd been down there to do my dancing and she was having a dinner party when I popped in afterwards to say hi. She said to me the next day, 'I can't believe you don't think you're eccentric. You come in to where people are sitting down to dinner and you do all this pirouetting and steps around and then you just flit off.' I was just showing them a few steps. I'm just getting the hang of it now. We're not up to tango yet. I'm doing samba and the salsa and lambada. My only unfulfilled ambition was to be a dancer. In my youth, Marge and Gower Champion were like Fred Astaire and Ginger Rogers and they danced in all those musicals of the fifties. I wanted to have the twirling skirts and throw my legs up. Because my parents moved around a lot I never got to do ballet. Anyhow, now I'm on the board of the Australian Ballet. I love it.

I need to work because I need to support myself but also I need to work because what else would I do? For example, I do enjoy being with my grandchildren. I've never been to McDonald's except to take away a hamburger until I had Matilda and Beatrice for the day. I said, 'What are we going to do for lunch?' Matilda said, 'Can we eat in McDonald's?' And I said, 'What do you mean, can we eat?' And she said, 'Oh, Mummy never lets us eat in McDonald's, we take the food away.' And I said, 'Oh, of course we can.' Well, we were there for two and a half hours in the playground and it was just so fabulous, they loved it. I sat there with my mobile phone and my books and the papers.

The upside of the unstructured life is just being able to choose what I want to do and do it. I like something I can be passionate about. It's quite a nice life except that it's a bit fragmented and disorganised. I'm speaking to the graduates at the University of Southern Queensland and I'm going to say that you can keep on changing. I'm still not quite sure what I'm going to be when I grow up. It's a question of all these different phases of your life. What is different for women in the new millennium is that you can recreate your life, not yourself. You're always yourself. I'm much more relaxed now than I was a couple of years ago.

I think it's a particularly female thing, that we are prepared to allow ourselves to be at sixes and sevens and to explore all these different directions. I think you have to continue to be bright and happy and available.

I don't think sex has ever been a major driving force in my life. In recent years, when I haven't had it, I haven't really missed it. I assume this is the big difference between men and women. I might think, I'd like to have a really good night with a bloke, but it's not solely for sex. I'd like someone to cuddle up to in bed. I like having my daughters to stay and cuddle up in bed. Although Genevieve recently said, 'Touch me, just lay a finger on me, and I'll thump you.' I said, 'For God's sake, Genevieve, I'm your mother.' I have the grandchildren to stay and have cuddles with them. What I would like is that feeling that there is one other human being barracking for you, for whom you're the most important person in the world and they are the most important. Funnily enough, in spite of all the things I've said about the marriage and about Leigh, I miss that sense of having another person there. Even if he wasn't keen on what I was telling him, he was sort of there, and in spite of all the badness, we did have lots in common. Common values and common interests and a lot of things that we mutually did like.

By far the toughest thing that I have had to cope with is the fact that, having remarried, Leigh has now applied to the Catholic Church for an annulment of our marriage. When he rang to tell me I was gobsmacked. And then I was very angry. I converted to Catholicism when I married him and I am still a practising member of the Catholic Church. We always took the children to mass every Sunday and my religion is very important to me. So I just can't believe he would do this.

If the annulment is granted, he can go to Communion and get married again in a Catholic Church. It all gets back to him living in sin in the eyes of the Church and not going to heaven. His grounds are that he had a dysfunctional childhood which led to an injudicious decision to marry me. I don't understand how an intelligent man can claim that a thirty-two-year marriage, which produced five children, should simply be annulled. Surely the Church has to rethink its attitude to divorce? It can't just go around annulling thirty-year marriages because they have failed. I am in shock over it.

I've never had my grand passion. It would be nice to think it was around the corner. My mother taught me never to give up. She found her grand passion late in life in the nursing home. She had some kind of undiagnosed problem which meant she was in a wheelchair, but it didn't stop her from falling in love with Bert, one of the chaps in the nursing home. I was Lord Mayor at the time and this urgent call came through from the head of Mum's nursing home. I was chairing a meeting of city engineers and water workers and I can still see the looks on their faces when I said into the phone, 'You've rung to tell me that my mother is misbehaving with a man? I have five children and you want me to worry about my *mother's* sex life? I mean, it's not as if she could get pregnant, is it?' My mother was adamant about Bert, and the nursing home said that if they were going to continue to behave in this manner they had to get married. So, against the wishes of other members of my family, she was married. I was her matron of honour and Damien, my son, gave her away. It was very sad that they didn't have all that long together, but at least my mother followed her passion.

As a wife, I tried. I think at the beginning I was a very good wife but unfortunately, as an eldest child, I needed to be appreciated and I felt unappreciated and neglected. So I then went off and found alternative sources of sustenance. They say that politics breaks up people's marriages, but people often go into politics because their marriages are not much good in the first place. Politics is very emotionally sustaining. In our family we had Leigh being emotionally sustained by neurosurgery, all that 'playing God' stuff, saving lives, and me being emotionally sustained by my children and the electorate. As a lover, I think I could be good. Lots of potential there, yet to be discovered. I still have that sense that there are always new things to be discovered. Basically, I'm optimistic. Usually in my life when one door closes, another one opens. I am always ready to walk through it. You have to keep on taking risks, that's what makes life exciting.

Update: Just before this book went to press, I rang Sallyanne to check on the state of the annulment. She told me that the tribunal had granted it. She has appealed the decision and is awaiting the result.

lunch, again

It ended with a lunch. Like most of the important things in my life. This time, however, lunch with the publisher was at the restaurant in my local pub. My shout.

There, sitting quietly on the table between us, was the manuscript. The child I was handing over to the adoptive parent.

'Well,' said the publisher, patting it affectionately, 'what did you write in your conclusion?'

'I don't believe in conclusions. They are too neat and often contrived. I believe in loose ends. You can't tie up people's lives like a neat brown-paper parcel with string and stickytape. It's the bits that don't fit in that are really interesting.'

He let it go.

We decided to order. After more chat and literary gossip, cornbeef and cabbage for him, sausages and mash for me, and towards the end of the first bottle of Sauvignon Blanc, he said, 'Come on, Susan, what can we learn from the women in this book? What do they have to teach us at the beginning of the new millennium?'

I could see that I wasn't going to escape from at least speculating about the answers to these questions. And in truth I did have some thoughts, however random or unconnected.

'Well, for a start,' I said, 'all of these women are outsiders.'

'Did you choose them because you feel that you are an outsider?'

'I was undoubtedly attracted to them because of that. But, you know, in reality all women are still outsiders. There may be those who think they have managed to penetrate the male world of power—some of those women who sit on corporate boards, for example. But many are only there as token women. They are chosen because they are most like the other men on the boards. As any self-respecting board needs at least one woman director on it, the women they choose tend to be those who think just like them. Sometimes a single-minded female outsider will be appointed by a male outsider but they usually do not seek to repeat the experience.'

'Can women really understand how power works in male circles?'

'I don't think they have any difficulty understanding it. But they are fooling themselves if they really begin to believe that they are "one of the boys" and can belong to it. They can go along with the culture but will be in serious trouble if they seek to radically change it.'

'But isn't the appearance of more women on the top corporate boards a sign that the old structures are beginning to break down?'

'It's an illusion. Unless at least half the board is female, and some of those women are not just faux-men, nothing will change.'

'So all women should know that they are outsiders?'

'Absolutely. They should celebrate it. There are definite benefits to being different. They should never try to pretend to see the world through male eyes. Those who do will lose any sense of themselves and won't know what they stand for. What is important is that we learn to accept these differences and change the world to accommodate them. There is no point in trying to pass for white if you are black. What you must insist on is that all cultural views are respected and that both male and female views of the world are represented.'

'Is so-called sisterhood dead?'

'If I am totally honest, the individuals who really helped me in my career were men. Certainly they were the ones in the positions of power to do so but it's also true that when women finally got into those positions, some of them actively worked against other powerful women getting there too. I think, like all sections of society who have for centuries been treated as "lesser", women often have difficulty helping anyone other than those who are way down the ladder and therefore no threat. Men are more used to tribal behaviour and have complex rituals of pay-offs and pay-backs. That's not to say that I and plenty of other women haven't tried to mentor or help others up the ladder. Envy is still a big problem in Australian culture.'

He smiled the smile of the secret society and moved the conversation along. 'Even though all these women have led very different lives and made very different choices, what do they have in common?'

'A huge number of characteristics.'

'Why don't you list them?'

'That sounds awfully like a conclusion.'

'Don't worry about the label.'

By now, of course, I was more than warming to the topic. I was passionate about these women. Even more so now, than when I had first talked to them. Once I started, I hardly paused for breath. Consider this my monologue.

Tall Poppies was the first of its kind. The intimate monologue. The warts-and-all narrative. What's now clear to me, seventeen years on, is that these women have continued to grow. Why? Because they are still not afraid of the truth, however unpalatable or threatening. I was much more focused and tough with them this time around because I knew them better. And I was more confident, more skilled. It's never easy to be asked the hard questions, the ones that poke and probe. And then to know that your words will be fixed in a book. You will be trapped in those pages. Forever. Takes guts to let someone do that to you. And trust.

I am a student of words. I believe they have the power to change lives. I believe they are the doorway to understanding culture. Fifteen years ago these women and their words helped us to understand our attitudes to many things, particularly success. Then the 'tall poppy syndrome' was unnamed, and therefore not widely understood. Now it is a national saying. Their stories helped to change our culture.

These women are ahead of the current culture. They have always been ahead of their times. They know there is a price to pay for that but they are willing to pay it. They have always been true to their own word. Always active players in their own narratives. Always invented their own lines. And their own lives.

If you want a life that's truly yours, then invent it. And live it.

If it all goes wrong, then learn the lessons and move on. Don't let the plot become boring.

Don't let the words tie you down or hem you in. Wife. What does that mean? Mother. Who defined it? Lover. Businesswoman. Artist. Create your own characters. Make up your own themes. Write a new script.

I love the fact that these women are all such great survivors. No, they're more than that. A survivor can be someone who is stoic and takes whatever is handed to them. These women are much more than that. They are bold. They have always been active participants in their own lives. Sure, lots of people have tried to chop them down. Some have succeeded. But the women never accepted it was the end. They just grew again. They always looked forward to the next flowering.

They are all battlers, but in very different ways. They each started out with major handicaps that could have been their crosses for the rest of their lives. I mean, they could have bored people to death with their tragic life stories. Pat was poor, Aboriginal and had a major mental breakdown. Did that mean she ended up on the scrapheap? With the greatest guts and courage she ended her marriage, took on the psychiatric profession and graduated in law. She never stopped taking on challenges. Even now she could sit quietly on the bench and rest on her laurels. She deserves it. She's worked hard for others all her life. It's taken her this long to realise that she doesn't have to prove herself to anyone. Ever again. But that has only given her the freedom to take on every kind of injustice. Now she doesn't seek anyone's approval except her own.

Maggie, too, was poor, always felt inadequate because she was no good at school and left at fourteen. Even though she married a couple of father figures, she always made her own way in terms of her career. When her modelling came to an abrupt end due to her weight gain, she didn't waste time whingeing and weeping about the cruelty of genetics, she simply reinvented herself as a marketer and finally as a fashion designer for women with larger figures. She never stopped trying to do the best and be the best and keep everyone happy in the process. Every time someone offered her a chance to start a new career, either in television or journalism, she took the risk and made a huge success out of it. The culture of celebrity meant that she lived her private life in the public gaze. Now in her sixties, she is living alone for the first time in her life, pleasing herself and celebrating it. That doesn't mean she is still not on the lookout for a sexy man.

Eve was a Jewish refugee who always felt out of step. The women's movement made her feel less alone and gave her the chance to be part of a cause; it gave her a chance to be passionate about something larger than herself. Even though on the surface she has lived a conservative married life, she has been far from the conventional wife. Never comfortable with full-time motherhood, she went back to work and created several businesses. She trades in none of the social smalltalk and niceties that women develop to ease communication. Nor does she wish to begin. Intellectual and not sexual pursuits excite her. She is a loner and she has stopped feeling guilty about it.

Robyn was born with an asthmatic condition that could still threaten her life. She has been a passionate teacher, singer, composer, writer, director and orchestrator of arts festivals. Nothing has ever stopped her pursuing her passions. She just 'becomes' it. She rockets herself into new universes and ways of being and thinking. She has chosen her sexuality, her relationship with the world, and she delights in everything she takes on. Because she believes in herself totally, her output and her energy continue to be amazing.

Fabian had a very privileged life and a well-known father whom she adored. When she took over his business, economic circumstances and her own inexperience catapulted it into receivership. She even had to sell her mother's house in order to stay afloat. Instead of drowning in a sea of guilt, recrimination and despair, she used her experiences to create a new career. She believes there is no such thing as failure, only lessons. If she really wants to achieve something she never takes 'no' for an answer. She seeks the help of others and finds a way. She is a visionary who never lets go of the dream. And the dream keeps expanding as her knowledge and her imagination find new pathways.

Anne always felt that in her family her needs came last, compared to those of her tribe of brothers. She saw herself as fat and ugly and never felt that her father approved of her. She gave up seeking approval and simply went ahead and invented her own life. She knows she is tough and strong, and even though she has experienced great success and failure, adoration and vilification, she always moves on to the next phase. She lives a diverse public life and an unconventional private life, both equally fulfilling.

Sallyanne thought she had fulfilled every girl's dream. She married a handsome doctor, had lots of nice children. When she found herself unhappy and trapped, she took any opportunity that came her way and ended up becoming Lord Mayor. Marriage wasn't so easy to get out of, so she threw herself into more politics. When it threw her out, she never gave up. Living alone in Paris as Trade Commissioner was not easy but she stuck it out. Politics continues to give her positions and take them away. But she is still hoping for a grand passion.

They have all led successful public lives but have been prepared to reveal their hurts, their vulnerability, their most intimate details. Their honesty, their truths, enlarge other people's lives, other people's sympathies. They give them a sense of life's possibilities. It is important not to let anyone force you into leading a little life. Particularly not yourself.

There is what George Bernard Shaw would call a 'life force' in these women. I think it stems from the knowledge that whatever happens to them, they are all now living their own lives. So many women lead the lives that their parents or their partners or their children expect them to lead. You can't wait for all these people to die before you start to live for yourself. This doesn't mean that you should lead a totally selfish life, a life not sensitive to the needs of others.

This is where I think some young women might have got it wrong. Freedom and equality are not just every woman's right, they are also a responsibility. You owe it to others to help them along the way. I don't see much evidence of a sense of the collective in younger women, but I think that's because of what happened in the 1980s. The economic model of 'greed is good' meant that the alternative philosophies of the 1970s seemed absurdly naive and idealistic. Economic rationalism as practised by both sides of politics has been a most pervasive cultural influence. Younger women are very keen to play an active role in determining the path of their own lives, but I don't see much passion for playing a part in the action of their times.

Causes other than their own individual ones don't appear to interest them. They are, however, showing great delight in their freedom and are determined to lead the lives they choose. They are confident. They are adventurous. They have a sense of their own power. And they live their lives on their own terms. Perhaps the need to come together to make big changes will come later in their lives, when they realise the limitations of individual effort. It takes a cause bigger than yourself to learn the power and excitement of the collective. They are certainly not the first generation of young women to stand on the shoulders of other women and not even know their names. Women's freedoms and fortunes are still vulnerable.

And what about me? Writing my first book about these women's lives certainly changed mine. It set me on a journey of finding my own path, from which I have never veered. Seventeen years on, and ten books and hundreds of women's stories later, I have left my academic career behind, moved to Sydney, and taken on the precarious life of the freelance journalist, broadcaster and writer. My parents, now dead, no longer need my help, and this has meant that even though I miss them, a lot, I no longer have to try to please them on the Big Days.

The women in this book, and in all my other books, have taught us that there is nothing more exciting, more exhilarating, than playing a part, however big or small, in the action of your times. If you don't like your life then invent one you do like. Again and again. The important factor is that you tell the truth about it, however difficult or painful, especially to yourself. If, in doing that, people berate you or label you, or find you too strong or too different or to difficult . . . well. The only answer is . . . tough.

The bottle was empty. The publisher had to go. He stood up and tucked the manuscript securely under his arm. I waved it goodbye. Lunch was over. Another day, another adventure. Yours and mine.

ACKNOWLEDGEMENTS

My thanks to Allen & Unwin: in particular Patrick Gallagher for the excellence of his lunches and his ideas; Colette Vella for her good humour, patience and skill as an editor; Sandy Webster and Rafael Rouco for their editorial and proofreading expertise; and Sonya Pletes and Nada Backovic for the wonderful cover photography and design.

Thanks also to Tim Curnow, for his rock solid support and professional advice.

The story 'Wedding Day' was first published in *Weddings & Wives*, edited by Dale Spender, Penguin, 1994. The stories 'Christmas Day' and 'Mother's Day' first appeared in the *Adelaide Review*.

And, finally, my deep-felt thanks to the women in the book, for having the courage to tell me the truth about their lives.